THE
RED WINES
OF BURGUNDY

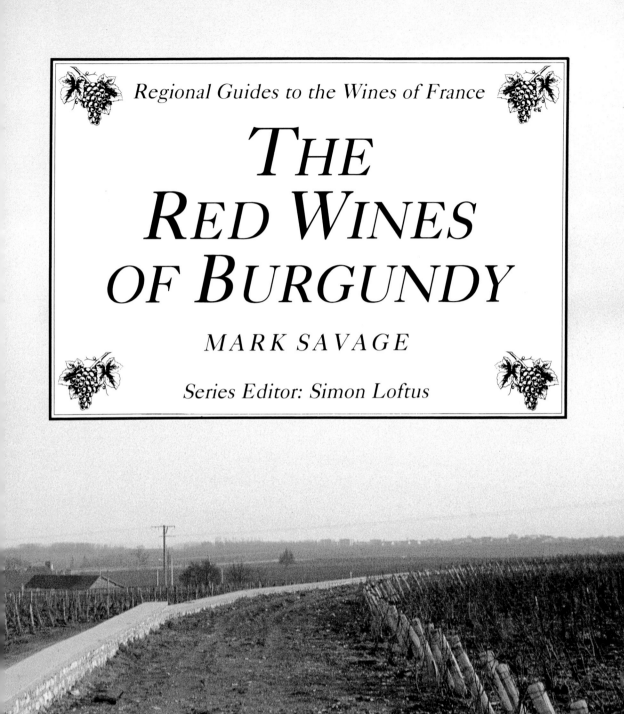

Regional Guides to the Wines of France

THE RED WINES OF BURGUNDY

MARK SAVAGE

Series Editor: Simon Loftus

OCTOPUS BOOKS

Half title page picture
*A cellar-worker uses steam and hot water to clean
barrels before use.*

Title page picture
*A stone cross stands sentinel over the Domaine de la
Romanée Conti's vineyards in Vosne-Romanée.*

First published 1988
by Octopus Books
Michelin House
81 Fulham Road
London SW3 6RB

ISBN 0 7064 3105 7

Printed by Mandarin Offset in Hong Kong

CONTENTS

Foreword 6

FOREWORD

"When young, the wine has a perfume that evokes soft fruits – raspberries, strawberries and cherries – sometimes with an underlying gamy quality that hints at the maturer characteristics to follow, which suggest rotten vegetables, woodland undergrowth and manure."

It sounds disgusting, the stench of decay, but wine lovers will echo Mark Savage's description of mature burgundy with even more unmentionable comparisons. The mystery is that such things can be said with enthusiasm, even with passion. Which proves two things: that burgundy is the most impossible of all wines to translate into words and that it evokes a more gut-felt response than any other.

The problem is compounded by the fact that experts disagree quite strongly about what fine burgundy should taste like. Some seek the finesse, the delicate complexity of the Pinot Noir grape. Others clamour for a rich, soupy depth of flavour that is perhaps more reminiscent of the bad old days, when a great deal of burgundy was blended with sturdier wines from the south, than the earthy subtlety which has always characterized the best of a wildly variable harvest.

Good burgundy is splendid; the rest is over-priced and unexciting.

Why should there be this extraordinary diversity of quality from vineyards which have been renowned for over a thousand years? It's a combination of two factors: the fickle unpredictability of the Pinot Noir grape (by far the fussiest of the great vine varieties of the world); and the minutely fragmented landholding pattern of the narrow, extended slope which is known as the Côte d'Or.

I am speaking of the heart of Burgundy, source of its greatest wines. The region as a whole extends from Chablis in the north (primarily known for its white wines) to the Beaujolais, which cheerfully satisfies an almost unquenchable world demand for quaffing wine, simple and immediate in its appeal. But the true Burgundy, the ancient duchy which once rivalled the court of the French kings, is centred on the town of Beaune and links a string of ancient villages, from Gevrey-Chambertin to Chassagne-Montrachet, which delineate a smaller world, intensely rural, proudly traditional, unbelievably complicated.

The aim of this book is to provide a reliable guide through the labyrinth. The task is made more difficult by the fact that the maze is always changing: dead ends suddenly become short cuts to the centre while formerly inviting paths are blocked. The guide must be better than a map, more like a survival kit – comprising compass, powerful torch, ball of twine, magnifying glass and (for real emergencies) a chainsaw to hack through the entanglements.

This may sound daunting, but those of an adventurous turn of mind will relish the challenges presented by Burgundy.

If you want to discover the best wines, you must get to know the growers and learn to disentangle the entwined cousinage of similar names. It was not always so. Until quite recently, most wine lovers felt content to recognize the labels of one or two decent *négociants*, the merchants who handled the vast preponderance of the region's wines. The *négociant* would buy his Pommard, for example, from a dozen or more small growers, blend their wines together (sometimes with the illegal addition of wine from a different village or even from outside Burgundy altogether) and mature the result in oak barrels in his cool stone cellars under the streets of Beaune or Nuits-St Georges. His expertise in this vital business of *élevage* (literally the bringing up or nursing of young wine until ready for bottling) allowed the small grower to get on with his own speciality: the daily agricultural tasks of the vineyard. The disadvantage of such a system is that the *négociant*'s aim tends to be consistency of quality and style from year to year; his skill as a blender inevitably blurs the individuality of the best wines that he handles. The personality of the grower, so strikingly evident in the greatest burgundies, is submerged in the *négociant*'s vat.

Not surprisingly, the best growers have been increasingly determined to control the destiny of their wine at every stage, from vineyard to consumer or importer. They have made the necessary investment in larger cellars; in expensive oak casks, bottling equipment and the like; and they have forgone the quick profit to be had by selling their wine to the '*négoce*' immediately after the vintage. Eventually they have reaped a greater reward because the customer has been happy to pay a high price for the apparent authenticity and 'cachet' of domain-bottled wines.

The result has been a proliferation of labels, undoubtedly adding to consumer confusion. Is it all worthwhile? As an enthusiast for fine burgundy I have to say 'yes', because the effort that I have had to make to learn the names, to discover the best producers, has been rewarded by the enjoyment of better wines than I ever tasted from the *négociants*. But it is also true that even the best growers make mistakes and that many others trade on the reputation of their region, to the frequent disenchantment of their customers.

At last there are signs that the *négociants* are fighting back. Several have been building up their vineyard holdings into sizable domains and now produce wines which can challenge the best of those from the individual growers. Others have realized that to buy wine from the small producers is to intervene in the process too late: increasingly they buy grapes and make the wine themselves. They advise the growers on planting, pruning and cultivation and they may well undertake the harvest. Such developments parallel the methods of a Californian winery and can lead to significant improvements in quality. It is a way forward for the future, a partnership with the growers which may help to diminish their traditional mistrust of the *négoces*.

Evolution has been slow but is now accelerating towards a better understanding of how true quality can be achieved, of how to produce (in often recalcitrant circumstances) that almost magical potion which challenges and delights wine lovers throughout the world. Demand exceeds supply, with the resultant temptation to cut corners and make a quick profit. The glamour of burgundy's international markets is to some extent in conflict with the rustic parochialism of the place itself, reflecting that other uneasy relationship, between the merchants and the producers. Such problems will always form the background to the pursuit of burgundy. For the real enthusiast they are part of its allure.

No book can fully explain a subject so densely interwoven with shifting patterns, but Mark Savage writes with the benefit of an international perspective: a passion for Pinot that stretches from the Côte d'Or to California. His lucid guide has the enormous advantage of being practical in its approach, up-to-date in its facts and judgments. It is the essential survival kit for explorers in the burgundian maze.

Simon Loftus 1988

BURGUNDY
AND ITS
RED WINES

*Autumn light casts a warm haze over the Côte d'Or
landscape. Behind the sleepy exterior of the village
of Chassagne-Montrachet, the cellars witness the
busy creation of a new vintage.*

INTRODUCTION

Bordeaux impresses by its scale and grandeur; the Rhône wins friends by its rich and spicy warmth; and the Napa Valley stuns its admirers with sheer energy and excitement. But for innumerable enthusiasts it is Burgundy which provides the finest red wines in the world: dazzlingly perfumed and flavoured, complex, subtle, irresistible. Even its most devoted admirers would have to admit, however, that at times it seems hopelessly disappointing, and overpriced into the bargain. Inconsistency is matched by geographical complexity: Burgundy would certainly win a prize for the world's most complicated wine region. The aim of this guide is to throw light into the labyrinth.

It has been said that it takes two to enjoy a bottle of Bordeaux but only one for a bottle of burgundy, suggesting that the first stimulates intellectual discussion, while the other is more selfishly sensual in its appeal. Bordeaux speaks to the brain, but burgundy sings to the heart. The former impresses with its austerity of style and its structure, with its classical balance, while the latter – less disciplined and less predictable – keeps us in suspense, fascinating us with its aromas, sometimes ethereal, sometimes animal, but nearly always enticing – unless of course the wine is showing us the sulky side of its character. The appeal of burgundy is romantic as opposed to classical, bohemian rather than conventional. It presents a greater challenge to the buyer by virtue of its sheer inconsistency. When great it is very great, but when poor it is awful. The grander it is, the shorter my tasting notes, for great wines are beyond words. Once tasted, though, the best burgundy can prove the most memorable of all wines.

The memory must be stretched between infrequent meetings. For it is not difficult, if provided with sufficient money, to go out and buy a great Bordeaux first growth, and there are people who will consume many such bottles every year. But few can hope to drink really great burgundy even once a year: in a lifetime, such wines may be counted in single figures. It is rare stuff indeed.

Red burgundy thus presents a thorny problem for the buyer, amateur or professional, since it cannot be cheap and is all too frequently poor. For those only half-interested in red wine it is, quite simply, best avoided. For red wine enthusiasts working to a limited budget, it is an area for occasional experiment, and failure must be taken philosophically. This is primarily the territory of the dedicated enthusiast, prepared to sacrifice the more normal luxuries and requirements of life and to spend a disproportionate amount of money in search of the unique experience provided by great red burgundy. Those who doubt whether they have the necessary perseverance are advised to stick to the safer and less expensive options provided by Bordeaux or the Rhône. Even enthusiasts should brace themselves for a rough ride over a road that is potholed with disappointments. There are no neat and tidy answers. The pursuit and enjoyment of fine red burgundy is rarely achieved without a measure of frustration.

But the rewards should make up for the dissapointments. Recent trends in the region suggest that the future will be better than the recent past in realizing Burgundy's true potential, with more and more good and genuine wine pushing the bogus and badly made out of the market place.

There is no attempt in this book to 'expose' individual producers or name those culprits responsible for damaging the reputation of Burgundy. Rather than leave the reader with a sour taste in the mouth, this book aims to further the appreciation of Burgundy's good wines by throwing light on the nature and problems of the region and its winemakers. There are no safe shortcuts, but I hope that the journey will prove a pleasurable and interesting one.

THE BIRTHPLACE OF GASTRONOMY
Because wine is so inextricably linked with food in France, and especially in Burgundy, no book on the wines of the region would be complete without reference to its cuisine. In France, the whole philosophy behind winemaking and drinking is connected with the food that is to accompany and enhance it. No other country has achieved this marriage with greater success, and no French region can make the same claim more convincingly than Burgundy. It is the place where one feels that fine wining and dining first began. It is here that *savoir-faire* comes to mean *savoir-boire-et-manger*, where instead of eating in order to live, people live in order to eat.

This reputation is old-established and well-founded. Major importance was attached to the construction of a grand kitchen by one of the Dukes of Burgundy in the fifteenth century. In 1677 Madame de Sévigné broke her journey one day at the Auberge Dauphin in Saulieu, and was able to record that, in addition to eating fish in meurette sauce, she drank so much good wine that she became tipsy for the first time in her life.

One reason for this reputation is the availability of excellent raw materials within the region. Bresse is celebrated for the finest chickens in France, Charolais beef is famous the world over, the Morvan is synonymous with fine ham, and freshwater fish crowd the waters of the Saône and the Rhône.

The gastronomic spirit of the region reaches its apotheosis at the time of *Les Trois Glorieuses*, three quintessentially Burgundian feasts that take place around the third weekend in November to coincide with the annual Hospices de Beaune wine auction. The wines made from parcels of good vineyards bequeathed by worthy Burgundians of the past are sold off in a blaze of publicity, with the proceeds going towards the running and upkeep of the Hospices de Beaune, the town's charitable hospital.

Of these feasts, the most famous, and perhaps pretentious, is that of the Confrérie des Chevaliers de Tastevin: a gargantuan banquet that takes place in the atmospheric splendour of the ancient Château du Clos Vougeot. This event may seem to outsiders, and not a few insiders, as somewhat bogus, yet it undeniably succeeds in its first aim of promoting the name of Burgundy throughout the world. In contrast to this piece of 'showbiz', designed for the self-glorification of the participants and the benefit of international public relations, there is the Paulée de Meursault, an earthy and authentic village party, given for the unashamed private pleasure of the locals and their friends, French or foreign. Between these two very different events is the third of the *Glorieuses*: a dinner in the *bastion* of the Hospices, taking place after the auction. To me, it is the Paulée which epitomizes the true spirit of the region and its people.

The same spirit is exemplified on a more individual level by a scene in a restaurant in Meursault one lunchtime. The local curé, a figure of generous girth and rosy complexion, whose considerable age betrayed no obvious decline in appetite for the good things of the region, made his appearance at 1 o'clock precisely. Neither requiring nor receiving a menu, he was promptly served with a kir, followed by a substantial four-course meal, lubricated by not just one, but two full bottles of white wine. His meal was concluded by coffee and a large glass of marc, the whole performance lasting exactly fifty minutes and bearing the undeniable signs of being a routine daily event. To the average Londoner, it might have seemed remarkable (whether bizarre, admirable or scandalous) but to a native *Bourguignon* such behaviour fails to evoke even the faintest flicker of an eyebrow.

A RECIPE FROM BURGUNDY

The wine of any good village and producer would partner this *Magret de Canard aux Baies de Cassis* well, but my preference would be for the elegance of a Chambolle-Musigny or Volnay rather than the power of a Pommard or Gevrey-Chambertin.

Magret de Canard aux Baies de Cassis
To serve 4

4 duck breasts, seasoned with salt and pepper
1 tablespoon vegetable oil
25 g (1 oz) butter
175 g (6 oz) fresh or thawed frozen blackcurrants
4 tablespoons Crème de Cassis
250 ml (8 fl oz) red burgundy
125 ml (4 fl oz) red wine vinegar
250 ml (8 fl oz) chicken or veal stock
1 tablespoon arrowroot slaked with a little water
1 bunch watercress

Melt the oil and butter in a heavy frying pan. Fry the duck breasts, skin side down, over a high heat for about 5 minutes until brown, then turn over and heat for a further 8 minutes. Remove the breasts and keep warm.

Simmer the blackcurrants in cassis for 1-2 minutes. (Fresh blackcurrants will take up to 10 minutes to become tender, and a little water may have to be added.)

Pour off all but 2 teaspoons of fat from the pan in which the duck was fried. Deglaze with the red wine, add the vinegar and reduce to about 4 tablespoons. Add the stock and bring to boil. Whisk in enough of the slaked arrowroot to make the sauce thick enough to coat a spoon lightly. Stir in the blackcurrants and check the seasoning. Keep warm.

Cut each duck breast into thin diagonal slices and arrange in a fan on each plate. Spoon over the sauce and garnish with watercress.

THE BURGUNDY REGION

In viticultural terms, Burgundy – when it is understood to include the Beaujolais, as in this book – cannot be regarded as a cohesive or homogeneous unit. This should not come as a surprise when one considers that it covers an area which stretches from the vineyards of the Yonne *département* in the north right down to those of the Rhône *département* in the south. Auxerre is one hundred and sixty kilometres from Paris, while Lyon is four hundred and sixty. That difference of three hundred kilometres (nearly two hundred miles) leads one to expect contrasts not simply in soil and climate, but also in things as fundamental as the very nature of the people. At one end, Burgundy can fairly be described as occupying the northern limit for the production of great red wine. At the other, the sunburnt roof tiles and sleepy afternoons of Beaujolais tell you that, if this is not exactly the South of France itself, it is at least the gateway to it.

LOCATION

Burgundy, then, is not one wine region, but several: the Yonne, Côte d'Or, Côte Chalonnaise, the Mâconnais, Beaujolais. (In terms of French *départements* we are concerned with the Yonne, Côte d'Or, Saône-et-Loire, and Rhône.) From a red-wine viewpoint, the Yonne is the least important of these, being an area that is best known for its white wine, Chablis. Pride of place goes to the Côte d'Or, which has produced all the great red wines that have made Burgundy world-famous. Indeed when talking of red burgundy, many people mean to refer exclusively to the wines of the Côte de Nuits and Côte de Beaune: the two slopes which together constitute the vineyards of the Côte d'Or. They stretch in unbroken sequence for approximately fifty kilometres (thirty miles) from Dijon in the north, through Beaune at the centre, down to Chagny in the south.

At this point the Côte Chalonnaise takes over, formed by a more fragmented chain of vineyards clustered around the villages of Mercurey, Rully, Givry, Montagny and Buxy. After a short break of mixed agricultural land, vineyards reappear in the Mâconnais district to the northwest of Mâcon itself. Finally the Beaujolais takes over and runs down to the very outskirts of Lyon. By this stage we are a long way, in every sense, from where we started and the wines of the Beaujolais can be regarded as having about as much in common with those of the Côte d'Or as they do with those of the Rhône. Few generalizations made about red Beaujolais apply to burgundy from the Côte d'Or. Apart from changes of soil and climate, and the character of the *vignerons* themselves, there is one change of major significance for red wines: the grape variety is no longer the Pinot Noir, but the Gamay. As we shall see, these two grapes do not give their best results in the same place.

HISTORY

Quite how and when the vine became established in Burgundy need not concern us in detail. Such study and argument is better left to the historian or archaeologist rather than the winedrinker. We do not need to know whether the strongest influence came from Phoenician Greeks bribing the local tribes with wine as they made their way up the Rhône from Marseille, or whether it was the Gaulish Celts themselves, as Pliny and Plutarch thought, who invaded Italy for the sake of its wine and then imported the skills for their own use at home. What is clear, however, is that the vine was well established in Gaul at least 2,000 years ago. The Emperor Domitian might be permitted a smile from his grave if he were to watch the European Community bureaucrats trying to make sense of the Common Agricultural Policy, for in AD 92 he himself had a wine-lake problem to solve in the Roman Empire and issued an edict to uproot all vines in the provinces. This may have been a protectionist measure on behalf of Italian winegrowers; in any case it never had much effect in central Gaul and was later repealed by the Emperor Probus. It was, though, an early sign of the chronic conflict between quantity and quality that confronts any wine industry, and is particularly significant with regard to Burgundy.

By the sixth century the influence of the monasteries on viticulture was becoming important. Burgundy owes much to the great abbeys of Cluny and Cîteaux in particular, the latter being responsible for the foundation of the Clos de Vougeot. An early indication of the superior quality of the region's wines is given by Petrarch's comment that the cardinals at

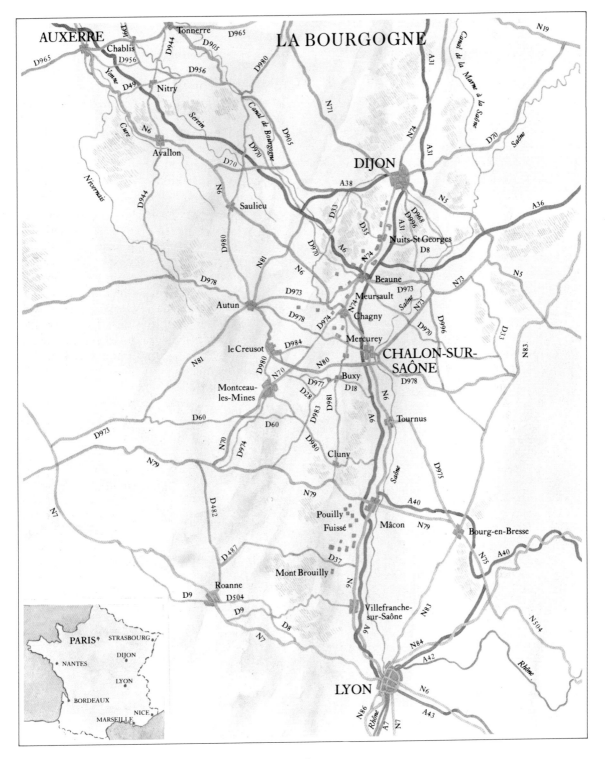

Avignon were reluctant to see the Papacy moved back to Rome lest it should deprive them of their beloved burgundy.

But it was not until the late fourteenth century that the fame of Burgundy was firmly established and its wine became the greatest in Europe. Under the Valois Duchy, the importance of the vine was clearly recognized, and wine became the chief item of commerce and agriculture. It was therefore vital to the wealth and power of a family whose influence at that time dominated France, and whose lands stretched from the Low Countries to Savoy.

It was the French Revolution and the Napoleonic laws of succession, however, that had the most drastic influence on the nature and development of Burgundy. These laws overturned the system of primogeniture (exclusive inheritance of the eldest son) in favour of splitting any inheritance between all the children concerned. While such a system may satisfy the principles of *égalité*, it does little for the economic growth and prosperity of a family estate, and to this day it remains the source of countless family quarrels in the region. It is also the main cause of hitherto viable agricultural units having to be dismembered and ultimately sold out of the original family altogether.

The large religious and aristocratic estates were thus carved up time and time again, and the subsequent fragmentation of land ownership has become the most charcteristic feature of Burgundian viticulture, as well as being the main cause of the enigmatic nature of its wines. It is also the major point of difference between it and Bordeaux, where individual holdings are much larger, and consequently where two bottles coming from the same vineyard appellation may be reasonably expected to taste the same.

<u>CLIMATE</u>

Burgundy is the world's northernmost producer of great red wine. This suggests, correctly, that the ripening of grapes is a marginal affair, and I believe that this is a crucial factor in the potential and actual success of the region. It has to be quickly admitted that the potential is not an easy one to realize: making great red burgundy is a tightrope act, in which memorable results are only achieved when great risks and great care have been taken. Top quality wine is rarely made by climate, soil and grape alone, and certainly never by a rigidly technological approach. To elevate winemaking from the realms of science to those of art requires imagination, experience and dedication. Nowhere are they more needed than in the Côte d'Or.

A mid-morning search for vegetables on market day in Nuit-St Georges provides
a reminder that, even in Burgundy, one cannot live by wine alone.

Not only does Burgundy, and particularly its northern end, have a climate that is barely sufficient for ripening red grapes, but it has chosen to try and exploit the most temperamental of grape varieties, the moody Pinot Noir, which, when tempted into other vineyards round the world almost always fails to perform with the grace, charm and elegance that it shows (albeit inconsistently) on its favourite patch of 'the Côte'.

The Burgundian climate is not all that different from the climate in Bordeaux, but the dividing line between success and failure is more marked and more frequently crossed. The northerly latitude of Burgundy is partly compensated for by a more continental climate than that of maritime Bordeaux: a climate of drama, with very cold winters followed by often torrid summers. What is clear is that the principal red grape of Bordeaux, the Cabernet Sauvignon, would not ripen in the Côte d'Or, and it is no accident that the Pinot Noir does not feature at all in Bordeaux or any of its satellites. The Cabernet Sauvignon is not a fussy grape, given enough heat and sunshine, but the Pinot Noir is a great deal less easy to please, if you are looking for real maturity as opposed to mere ripeness. It seems to need stress from its climate. By the time one is as far south as Mâcon, it is time to abandon it in favour of the Gamay.

SOIL

In the international search for an explanation as to why one vineyard or region produces greater wine than another, the French tend to focus attention on the soil. Indeed, France so respects the influence of soil that it has based its entire *Appellation Contrôlée* system on it. To do the French justice, it is not simply a question of soil type that matters, but rather the combination of soil and micro-climate which together form the environment in which grapes mature and acquire character. This is what the French mean when they speak of *terroir*.

Is it right that so much importance should be attributed to the geographical formation and the actual earth of a vineyard? There are many outside France who prefer to play down the soil aspect and pay more attention to the techniques of winemaking. Even those who are certain of the importance of the soil have to admit they are not absolutely sure as to how and why it has its influence. Talk of *terroir* and trace elements, of drainage and soil structure, and you are soon in the realm of the inexplicable and mysterious, as far as verifiable effects on fermented grape juice are concerned. The data are too imprecise and uncertain for scientific analysis of a wine's greatness. Those who find this uncertainty uncomfortable may be tempted to look elsewhere for the real reasons, to more easily measurable factors such as light and heat and technical skills. Even if the theoretical argument cannot be fully resolved, the soil protagonists of France are in a strong position when it comes to the practical side of things: their wines are still the envy of the world. It may, therefore, be worth a slightly more detailed look at the *terroir* of Burgundy, to try and discover what gives its wines their style, complexity and uniqueness.

In the Côte d'Or, the dominant soil elements are limestone and marl. Because of the importance of drainage, the best vineyards all lie on the slopes. The best of all, for Pinot Noir, will be found half-way up the slope (on the *mi-côte*), for that will be where the best soil combinations are achieved. Too high up and the soils will be too light, while low down the drainage will be poor. Where the soil is predominantly light and calcareous, with more lime than clay, the Chardonnay grape is preferred to the Pinot Noir. Hence the greatest white burgundies are found on the Côte de Beaune. Conversely it is on the somewhat redder and richer soils of the Côte de Nuits that the Pinot Noir performs best.

The Côte de Nuits and Côte de Beaune might easily (taking a lead from the Northern Rhône's Côte Rôtie) have called themselves, respectively, Côte Brune and Côte Blonde, for even a cursory glance across the vineyards as one drives through them reveals a visible difference in colour of the topsoil. The paler and poorer-looking soil is more suitable for white Montrachet than red Chambertin.

Another factor that may influence the choice of grape comes not from the actual soil, but from the exposure of the vineyard. A glance at the map will reveal a small but perceptible difference in the inclination of the Côte de Nuits and the Côte de Beaune, for the former looks due east for the most part, while the latter turns more to the southeast. The significance of this lies in the fact that the earlier the sun gets at the vineyard, the quicker it will warm up, encouraging ripeness and drying off any of the rot-producing moisture that may damage the grapes. This is justly considered to be an important factor in the Côte d'Or and in a marginal ripening year it could make all the difference between success and mediocrity. (1980 was such a year: the Côte de Nuits produced wines clearly superior to those of the Côte de Beaune.)

*Oak barrels, both new and not-so-new, are a vital ingredient in Burgundian winemaking.
The skill of the cooper may be as significant as the source of the oak itself.*

But our investigation of Burgundy must extend beyond the Côte d'Or, which is a small fraction of the whole area, albeit the most significant as regards quality. Moving south of Chagny, we find ourselves in the Côte Chalonnaise, an area of much more irregular conformation than the Côte d'Or. The vineyard appellations here do not follow each other without a break, but are separated, giving a more polycultural character to the countryside. In Mercurey, the best village of the Côte Chalonnaise for red wine, the subsoil is not dissimiliar to that found further north, and the wine at its best easily rivals the village wines of Nuits-St Georges.

Further south again we find the Mâconnais, whose red wines need not detain us long, since they lack the finesse of those of the Côte d'Or and the charm of those of the Beaujolais. The limestone soils here are more suited to white wine production.

Finally we come to the Beaujolais district. As I have already said, there are good reasons for treating this region quite separately from the rest of Burgundy, from a viticultural point of view. Its inclusion in books about Burgundy is something of a geographical convenience. It does, though, present us

with a perfect example of the importance of matching grape variety to *terroir*. Here the grape variety used is the high-yielding Gamay, outlawed on the Côte d'Or, while the Pinot Noir is completely absent. The soil, too, has changed: it is now characterized, at its best, by decomposed granite. In volume terms Beaujolais accounts for as much, if not more, than all the other districts of Burgundy put together. With its wine we have moved from the complex, subtle thoroughbreds of the Côte d'Or to the ultimate in uncomplicated winedrinking pleasure. It demands the attention of neither the brain nor the heart, but quenches the thirst and lifts the spirit.

This brief consideration of the climate and soil in Burgundy provides us with no explanation for the style of the wines. Even the most exhaustive studies would not help us to arrive at a definitive conclusion as to why the wines have their special distinction. There is no magic formula for great wine. You might also say that there is no great secret either. You simply need a site that has a winning combination of soil and climate, and a man with enough intelligence and experience to realize the full potential of the grapes that grow there.

16

VITICULTURE –
GROWING THE GRAPES

A major contrast between the north and south of the Burgundy region is to be found in the two quite different grape varieties that dictate the style and quality of their respective wines. Northern Burgundy produces the world's greatest Pinot Noir wines, while the Beaujolais district in the south does the same for the Gamay. It was not always so.

In fact, the Gamay grape has long been associated with the north of Burgundy. There is a village of that name between St Aubin and Chassagne-Montrachet, territory from which it is now firmly excluded (except when blended with a third Pinot Noir for sale under the appellation Bourgogne Passetoutgrain). During the nineteenth century the vineyards near Dijon were given over entirely to the Gamay, whose inexpensive wines were much in demand in the city. Throughout the Côte d'Or, Gamay covered most of the cultivated vineyard area. In spite of numerous attempts to curb and even ban its presence throughout the centuries, the Gamay has played an important traditional role in Burgundy, as a large-volume producer of wine for everyday consumption. Only in the modern era has it been successfully restrained, and much of the credit for this must be given to the *Appellation Contrôlée* laws, which have designated the permitted grape varieties for each area. This appreciation of the need to match grape and soil lies at the heart of France's reputation as the world's greatest wine producer.

No doubt the task in Burgundy was made much easier by the growth in European prosperity and a worldwide demand for the best that France had to offer. In the past, times were much harder and it may reasonably be supposed that the Gamay was there, not by virtue of greed or any desire to defraud, but out of sheer economic necessity. It was all very well for the Dukes of Burgundy to insist on Pinot Noir – they were wealthy enough to afford the best – but most people in those days wanted affordable red wine to drink without delay. The market is now influenced by drinking habits, aspirations and snobberies of restaurant-goers and private collectors in London and Los Angeles, Toronto and Tokyo, Dallas and Düsseldorf. It now pays to plant Pinot Noir, and pays handsomely: no other fine wine region is faced with a demand so far in excess of supply.

THE GAMAY

The Gamay Noir à Jus Blanc, to give it its full name, may be a major grape in France in terms of volume production, but as regards actual quality it is fashionable rather than noble. In the Beaujolais district it accounts for ninety-eight per cent of the vineyard area. Its *raison d'être* is its ability to produce relatively light and uncomplicated, but nonetheless satisfying red wine at a reasonable price. In doing so, it has established itself as the ultimate 'carafe' or 'jug' wine. It is definitely not designed for serious deliberation and candlelit dinner tables. Just as the Sauvignon Blanc grape can give us crisp and refreshing young white wines, so we look to the Gamay for a thirst-quenching red. Indeed the obvious fruit, acidity and youthful charm of Beaujolais give it the attributes more normally associated with a white wine and it may be no accident that its success has come during a period that has witnessed a white-wine boom worldwide. (One of the better Beaujolais *crus*, Côte de Brouilly, can even smell more like a Sauvignon Blanc than a Gamay.) These attributes have been emphasized by the system of vinification normally adopted in Beaujolais – a form of *macération carbonique* (see pages 20 and 69) – that almost exaggerates the fruitiness of the Gamay itself.

But there is another side to the coin, and *terroir* plays its part here too. The Gamay can be made to work harder on certain soils, notably in the light, decomposed, schistous granite found on the hillsides of the Haut-Beaujolais. Here the vines are trained and pruned *en gobelet*, as individual bushes: the permitted yields are lower: and the wine itself is not vinified almost overnight for consumption within the year. The best wines of the Beaujolais show that the Gamay is capable of ageing well and also expressing individual characteristics that reflect a particular locale. Oddly, with bottle age, the wine can take on a style and flavour that is strongly reminiscent of Pinot Noir, and a mature ten-year-old Moulin-à-Vent or Morgon from a good vintage may be almost impossible to distinguish from a Côte de Beaune. On the heavier, less well-drained soils of the Bas-Beaujolais, the vines are grown on wires by the Guyot method, yields are higher, the wines are less remarkable and less capable of longevity. This is 'Nouveau' territory.

Pinot Noir

"Good Pinot Noir is rare as hen's teeth" said an American winemaker to me one day, expressing his exasperation at the difficulties posed by this variety. An appreciation of its nature and its problems is vital to any attempt at understanding the red burgundy enigma. In contrast to the Gamay, the Pinot Noir is one of the world's classic grape varieties. But it is also one of the most unpredictable and fussy, presenting a constant challenge to both grower and winemaker alike. In this aspect it is far less accommodating than its white counterpart in Burgundy, the obliging and fashionable Chardonnay.

Pinot Noir is classed as a 'noble' grape, yet all too often it exhibits signs of ill-breeding. Bad blood seems to have sullied the strain and compromised its aristocratic aspirations. Or, more likely perhaps, it is an ancient and primitive grape that is prone to betray its 'wild vine' origins when they are least wanted. It has none of the confident and seemingly natural sophistication of the Cabernet Sauvignon. It has a long history of genetic instability, and is so subject to mutation that its proprietors are unlikely to be able to identify positively all the strains in their vineyard. (Theoretically it is possible to identify more than 1,000 different clones.) It is capable of showing an

Ripe Pinot Noir grapes set against the red soil of the Côte de Nuits.
The traditional wicker pannier is normally replaced now by the plastic tub.

PINOT NOIR

GAMAY

identifiable varietal character, but this is desperately easy to lose, either through overcropping on the vine, or by overchaptalization and overblending in the vat. When young, the wine has a perfume that evokes soft fruits – raspberries, strawberries and cherries – sometimes with an underlying gamy quality that hints at the maturer characteristics to follow, which suggest rotten vegetables, woodland undergrowth or manure.

To produce these characteristics, Pinot Noir almost certainly requires a marginal ripening climate. It is by nature an early ripening variety, and for this reason it is less successful in a warm climate than in one where it needs to struggle. Pinot Noir grapes that are merely ripe, as opposed to mature, tend to make a coarse and clumsy wine, as Californian producers have found out. But this marginal ripening environment is only one of its demands.

Low yield is always a key factor when it comes to quality, and this is particularly true of the Pinot Noir. Just as economic reasons lay behind the widespread use of the Gamay in Burgundy's past, so in more recent times, the search for a better financial return, whether motivated by greed or necessity, has led to the use of more productive clones. With a capricious grape, much subject to virus attack, and in a marginal ripening climate, the borderline between success and failure has always been narrow. Furthermore, now that there is insufficient wine to satisfy the market, the temptation is to try and produce more. The wine producer must make a conscious decision between opting for quantity or quality.

The real key to grape quality lies in selection in the vineyard. The best proprietors will have identified and bred from their best plants over a long period of time. Their system of selection 'in the mass' (*sélection*

massale) is far from precise and relies on experience, always an invaluable weapon in the wine producer's armoury. Any well-established Pinot Noir vineyard in Burgundy is likely to have perhaps a dozen or so different varieties of Pinot Noir vines. Some plants may indeed produce exceptional wine, but in such minute volume that it would have to be unacceptably expensive. Other vines will be prone to serious overproduction, and if the selection in the vineyard swings too much in their direction, the resulting wine will lack the concentration necessary for fine flavour and structure. Some compromise is therefore essential between the higher yielding, thinner skinned varieties and those that are harder to work and produce less wine, but contribute vital refinement and power. Actual variety aside, the other *sine qua non* is the need for a good proportion of deep-rooted old vines, whose grapes produce wines with good natural alcohol, acidity and extract.

When quality in a vineyard deteriorates, the finger of suspicion is generally pointed at the clones in use. But the reason for poor quality is more frequently found in overcropping. In spite of the laws that stipulate maximum permitted yields for every Burgundian appellation, official derogations of the law now seem to be the rule rather than the exception, and actual yields have become dangerously high in some cases. The ideal approach includes a good selection of plants, with a proportion of old vines, and a carefully controlled yield achieved through a vigorous pruning policy in the vineyard. Too many growers simply assume that nature will do the pruning herself in the form of poor flowering, a hard frost or a bad hailstorm. Viticultural expertise and sagacity, when harnessed to a favourably exposed and drained slope, are the key to the production of great red wines.

VINIFICATION –
MAKING THE WINE

Fermentation is a spontaneous natural reaction: given the presence of yeast and sugar, grapes will turn into wine, or perhaps into wine vinegar. As yeast is present on grape skins, and sugar in grape juice, little or no help is required from man. But to make great wine is more complicated. Once nature has played her part in terms of plant, soil and climate, then it is up to man to take over and make the most of nature's raw materials. Great wines have their origins in the vineyards, it is true, but it is in the subsequent vinification that their potential is either realized or destroyed. There are certain ground rules, but the variety of ways in which these rules can be applied or misapplied by each producer is yet another factor behind the huge quality variations of red burgundy. In Bordeaux, the procedures followed by one *cru classé* in the Médoc are very likely to be almost identical to those practised by its neighbour. In Burgundy, everyone has his own house style, his own formula for vinification. Another difference is that in Bordeaux the *cépage* – grape variety or varieties – tends to dominate in the wine, while in Burgundy the *terroir* can be given a higher profile if the winemaker allows.

Vinification takes place in two stages: first the fermentation of the grape must, and secondly the *élevage* of the wine itself, the process of bringing it up until it is ready to be sold or consumed.

MAXIMUM FRUIT, MINIMUM TANNIN

Not surprisingly the rules that apply for a wine designed to be drunk very young are not the same as those for wines that deserve longer ageing. In Beaujolais over fifty per cent of the production is now made as a *primeur* designed for consumption by the Easter following the vintage, if not by Christmas, and most of the balance that remains within the following twelve months. The distinguishing feature here is the use of a modified version of the vinification system known as *macération carbonique*. The essential difference between this method and the normal one is that the grapes are not crushed before being put into the fermentation vat. The aim of this whole-berry fermentation is to maximize the fruit flavour and minimize the extraction of tannin. (Taken a stage further, with carbon dioxide being pumped into closed vats, this system has grown rapidly in popularity in areas such as the Midi, in response to demand for wines of charm, suitable for early consumption.) Even if the system reduces the wine's ageing potential, it may be defended on the grounds that it accentuates its appeal enormously, and accelerates development. As a formula for maximum cashflow, therefore, it is an absolute winner, and to judge by worldwide sales, it is also extremely popular with customers. Fresh, forward fruit flavours are in fashion now, not stalky, tannic wines that need years to soften into a state of smooth maturity. This is one of the major reasons for the huge popularity of Beaujolais and the region's current prosperity. As for *élevage*, that is an irrelevance, as the wine has been finished off (*acheté, bu et pissé*) before most Côte d'Or burgundies have been even bottled. There are few exceptions to this rule now in the Beaujolais district, although it is still possible to find producers in the better *crus* such as Moulin-à-Vent who give their musts a longer *cuvaison* (vatting time) than most, in order to extract more tannin from the skins and thus give their wines a greater potential for ageing.

THE PURSUIT OF PERFECTION

Further north the picture is more serious and inevitably more complicated. Technical and aesthetic perfection is consequent on perfect balance of all the wine's components: the winemaker should be searching for the formula that will give him this, while at the same time allowing him to get maximum expression from the grape and its *terroir*. In Burgundy, nature does not deal the same hand of cards every year, so the winemaker has to be prepared to use different corrective strategies to win the round.

Most grapes for most red wines can be treated quite roughly (unlike those for white wine), but yet again the Pinot Noir is an exception: it needs to be handled with unusual care. The essential difference between the vinification of red grapes and white grapes lies in the fact that for red wine the juice must remain in contact with the skins as it ferments, to extract tannin and colour. Rot must therefore be avoided at all costs, as unhealthy grapeskins will give unwelcome flavours to the must. This problem is significant in a climate such as that of Burgundy, where

It may well be 2 a.m. but there is little time for sleep during the vintage. This cellarman reveals the dirty and exhausting side of winemaking as he empties a fermentation vat in the Beaujolais district. The grape must has been run off to complete its transformation into wine elsewhere in the cellar.

hail and rain are ever-present dangers.

If rot has contaminated the grapes the winemaker is faced with a dilemma: he needs to extract colour from the skins without simultaneously contaminating the juice with the flavour of the rot. If he runs the juice off the skins too quickly in his attempt to avoid this, he will deprive himself of the depth of colour that results from more prolonged maceration. (The 1983 vintage presented a vivid illustration of this problem.) The solution lies in rigorous rejection of any rot-affected grapes: "*Il faut trier, trier et encore trier*" (sort through over and over again) says Michel Lafarge of Volnay. Good wine depends on careful selection at all stages of the process.

In another respect, too, the Pinot Noir grape poses problems to the winemaker. While a really deep colour is neither vital nor even particularly typical of red burgundy, the producer knows that the majority of his customers will not expect to pay a high price for a glass of what may seem to be no more than a rosé. It has been said that the first duty of a red wine is to be red, and it is perhaps the desire of the producer to please his client in this respect that has led to many of the past abuses of the wine, when robust red wines from the Midi or North Africa were blended into 'fine' burgundy. We are now witnessing, I believe, a

21

move towards more honest burgundy, but the irony is that the truth may be less palatable than was the fiction. The old deceptions were not conceived out of any real desire to defraud the consumer, but rather out of the natural commercial law of the market place which decrees that the consumer should be given what he or she wants. But fashions have changed, and blending in wines from other regions has ceased to be part of professional winemaking. Every year sees a new wine scandal erupt somewhere or other, and the public have become highly sensitive to possible fraud. This in itself is healthy, but it will not do anything to remove the disappointments involved in making and buying red burgundy. The problems will not go away.

As already stated, in Burgundy each producer has his own cherished interpretation of the rules of wine-making. The principal areas of flexibility concern destalking (*égrappage*), fermentation, temperature, and length of vatting (*cuvaison*). The traditionalist who aims for maximum longevity will retain a large proportion of the stalks and vinify the juice in contact with the skins for a month or more, while the majority of winemakers, now catering for a market that needs wines to drink quickly, will opt for total *égrappage* and a much shorter *cuvaison*.

The area of vinification that causes the most controversy is the question of chaptalization: the addition of ordinary refined sugar to the must during fermentation. This is done in order to raise the alcohol level in the wine (yeasts, feeding on sugar, produce alcohol). Along with overproduction in the vineyard, it is this practice, when abused, which is most damaging to the wine. Used judiciously it can even contribute to a wine's complexity, but old habits die hard, and overchaptalization remains a serious problem in Burgundy. It masks the purity of the Pinot Noir fruit, obliterates the wine's individuality and upsets rather than improves its balance, leaving a fiery taste in the drinker's throat. The French obsession with high alcohol levels in wine is deep-seated, but this is another area in which recent developments encourage those of us who think that thirteen degrees of alcohol is inappropriate for the style and balance of Pinot Noir.

THE EFFECT OF OAK

For the *élevage* ('nursing' the wine during its maturation in cask) much of the work is routine: the wine must periodically be racked off the lees (taken off its sediment) and the barrels regularly topped up. The primary or alcoholic fermentation should be followed by the secondary, malolactic fermentation, which smooths out and improves the wine's balance.

An area of particular interest in *élevage* concerns the use of small new oak casks, or *barriques*. Traditionally, red wines in the Côte d'Or are aged for between one and two years in these 228-litre casks. They are coopered from seasoned oak drawn from French forests such as those of the Limousin, Allier or Nevers. When used wisely, the character of great wine can be much enhanced by new oak in the cellar. It can add richness, spice and overall complexity. (On wines from lesser grapes and from less fortunate vineyards, such extra embellishments are a waste of time.) But the balance is critical, for the oak can easily dominate the fruit. It is, to some extent, a question of taste and style, but the use of oak should never be heavy-handed. The proportion of new casks to those that have already served a few seasons in the cellar is an important matter of judgement for each vintage, and each winemaker.

In recent years there has been a good deal of justified grumbling about the quality of red burgundy. Are production methods at fault, or is it simply that a misconception exists as to the true character of this wine?

There remains a widely held view that red burgundy should be heavy whereas, if it is genuine, it is nearly always lighter than red wine from Bordeaux, let alone the Rhône. Imitations of burgundy from California, South Africa, Australia and South America all serve to perpetuate the myth of 'big burgundy'. This is not to defend some of the disgracefully thin wines that have provoked the discontent of many consumers and damaged the region's reputation. But talk of a significant difference between the 'big' wines of the good old days and those produced by current methods is largely misconceived. If there has been a decline in quality since the war, this is the result of excessive yields rather than of vinification. There is certainly far more control and understanding nowadays of the whole progress of turning grapes into wine. Disaster vintages seem to have been virtually eliminated and something reasonable can now be produced even in the wettest or coldest year.

There is, in fact, something of a revolution afoot in Burgundy at present. A new generation of wine producers is struggling for a regional renaissance: the return of real quality, honest winemaking and a full exploration of the unique potential of Burgundy. We shall examine this development more closely by looking at the producers themselves and the current structure of the trade in Burgundy.

THE BURGUNDY WINE TRADE

A new sense of direction is apparent throughout Burgundy. The major impetus for this has come from within Burgundy's wine trade, and it coincides with the rise to prominence of the growers. Strange as it may seem to outsiders, the growers have not always been the principal factor in the Burgundy equation, and this was one reason for the indifferent quality of much burgundy in the past.

The four main participants in the Burgundy wine trade are as follows:

(1) The *vignerons* or *propriétaires-récoltants*: men and women who grow the grapes and, for the most part, make the wine, even if they do not necessarily bottle it themselves.

(2) The *négociants-éleveurs*: merchants, who are often also vineyard-owning growers and winemakers in their own right, who buy wines in quantity, blend them on a commercial scale and market them all over the world.

(3) The *courtiers*: brokers, who play a much less visible, but vital, role as a link between growers and merchants.

(4) The *coopératives*: wine cooperatives, so important to European winemaking in general, are of negligible importance on the Côte d'Or, but significant in volume terms in the Mâconnais and the Beaujolais.

Prior to 1970, up to ninety-five per cent of the wine on the Côte d'Or passed through the hands of the *négoce*, as the *négociants-éleveurs* are familiarly known. They had gained their importance as a direct result of the minute fragmentation of the vineyard holdings, for not only is it difficult to vinify wine in very small lots, but it is even harder to set about commercializing it. Thus the large merchants were needed by the small growers. The arrival of domain bottling, in which the grower makes, bottles and sometimes sells his own wine, has precipitated a major shift in the balance of power. Nowadays, over

In the smart new underground cellars of Domaine Rion in Premeaux, near Nuits-St Georges, Daniel Rion inspects a sample of young wine drawn by pipette from one of his new oak casks.

fifty per cent of red burgundy is being bottled at the domain on which it was produced, and around a third of the total is being sold by the individual producers themselves. This has put the growers in the driving seat – and the merchants on the defensive.

The 'wicked' merchant has traditionally been branded as the villain of the piece and it is in the grower's interests to perpetuate this myth. The truth is less clear, for there are good and bad merchants, just as there are good and bad growers. It would be naive to think that either was immune from the temptations presented by a commodity on which fraudulent profits can easily be made.

THE GROWER'S DOUBLE REWARD

The success of any business depends on the presence of incentives. If demand for a product is so strong that it will sell at any price, irrespective of quality, then it is inevitable that some producers (or merchants) will make hay while the sun shines. It is equally clear that consumers cannot be fooled for ever, that clouds will appear and that the sun will set. Fortunately there are healthy incentives also, which motivate producers towards long-term quality and reputation rather than short-term gain. It is this that lies at the heart of the current renaissance in Burgundy, for the growers, in liberating themselves from contractual ties to *négociants*, have discovered the rewards of selling their own wine at a price that reflects its quality. They no longer make their wine in the knowledge that it is doomed to end in the blending vat, mixed in with the inferior product of an incompetent or less fortunate neighbour, or indeed 'cut' with wines of even more ignominious origins. Instead they can devote themselves to extracting the maximum character and finesse from their grapes and their *terroir*. They now enjoy the double reward of pride and profit.

The opportunities open to the grower are steadily increasing on another front, too: consumers nowadays like to cut out the middlemen and beat a direct path to the producer's door. The effects of this may not be so welcome, as the producer will find it much easier to defraud the amateur than to defraud the professional broker or merchant he had to deal with in the past. He, too, benefits by cutting out the middlemen, for he can charge the customer a high price. And if he is unscrupulous, it is all too easy for him to dispose of his less successful creations by dubious means. What he offers the passer-by to taste may differ from what he puts into the boot of his car, but the anger of the tourist when he gets home will hardly

Georges Duboeuf, the best-known merchant in Beaujolais, gets his nose into a grower's sample.

worry him as much as the anger of a broker upon whose long-term confidence his livelihood depends. When life gets too easy, people get lazy. Fair profit turns swiftly to greed. If the growers abuse their current position by producing inferior wine, which they market dishonestly, they can be sure that the pendulum will swing back towards the honest merchants.

At present, however, there is plenty of evidence to suggest that the growers, far from cheating, are fully aware of the great opportunity that is there to be seized. The apparent renaissance in quality that is taking place in Burgundy can be traced firmly to the door of the grower, and his rise to power is proving to be excellent news for the consumer.

THE MERCHANT'S TALE

Where, one may well ask, does this leave the merchants? They have played a major role in spreading the fame of Burgundy throughout the world. They have the ability to vinify, blend, mature, bottle, and finally to commercialize the wines in a manner not open to the small grower. The role of an *éleveur* is an expensive one. Cellar equipment grows more and more sophisticated and expensive by the year, new oak barrels have to be purchased (currently £200 or 2,000 francs each), staff nowadays enjoy good wage levels and lengthy paid holidays, and then there is the cost of financing large stocks of wine. The merchant's strength lies in his ability to shoulder such burdens, most of which are well beyond the budget of individual growers. In origin, merchants are growers who have become so successful they have had to expand beyond their family holdings in order to meet the demand for their wines. They know the grower's end of the *métier* very well, and they have the extra strength of being able to offer their clients a wide range of wines from useful appellations. Their weakness, however, lies in the fact that their wines tend to lose the *typicité* of their appellations as a result of heavy-handed winemaking on a large scale. The different wines thus give the impression of having little more than different labels, rather than of being a reflection of individual *terroirs*. This lack of distinction and individuality is the commonest criticism of the merchant's wines.

The merchant has his reasons, though: he has to take a very different view of the market from the small grower. Individuality and vineyard character may well be a lower priority for the merchant trying to keep his customers than consistency and stability. As a result, heavy filtration is common and pasteurization is not unknown in the premises of large merchants, while such practices are rare or non-existent in the cellars of small growers. Merchants' wines receive much more treatment at every stage of their *élevage* than do growers' wines, and it is this extra handling which is so dangerous when dealing with naturally fragile wines from the Pinot Noir grape. If there is a single reason why consumers should think twice before buying *négociant*'s wines, it is that they may simply have less character.

Not surprisingly, many *négociants* are being obliged to reconsider their role in the face of this threat to their survival. For some this means putting greater emphasis on promoting mass-market proprietary brands of table wines whose origins are far removed from Burgundy. If the merchant concerned is already famous for his burgundy, he hopes his name on the label will help sell the brands, while the customer may think (erroneously) that he is drinking some form of declassified burgundy itself. (In reality, no such surplus exists, or if it does, it shouldn't.) Other *négociants* may assume a role closer to that of broker, rather than blender and stockholder. But the best merchants will survive intact, and emerge stronger than ever from the process. The reasons for their existence still hold and they can continue to perform a most valuable role in a trade that needs them. But they will need to perform that role very well if they are to survive against the new quality competition from the best of the growers and the brokers who work for them on world markets. The biggest problem for the merchants is simply that the sources of their best wines have dried up. It will get harder still in the future for them to find good wines,

and when they do find them, they will be made to pay much more for them than in the past. From a quality perspective, the consumer must benefit from this development. The wines may cost more, but if a price has to be paid for the resurrection of fine burgundy, then so be it. The consumer will have a much better chance of getting authentic wines of real individuality — hence value for money.

COURTIER: ÉMINENCE GRISE

The *courtier* or broker continues to perform his useful backstage role much as he has always done. That role is one that can only be performed by someone with the most intimate knowledge of all the individual growers, no matter how small, in his field of operation. Not surprisingly, therefore, *courtiers* are almost invariably local men and it is a profession that is commonly passed down from generation to generation within a family. Such knowledge is not acquired overnight. Their job is to put the right grower in contact with the right merchant. Not only must the *courtier* know all the growers and the style of their wines, but he must also be aware of the requirements of each individual merchant. Thus if a *négociant* in Beaune is looking for twenty hectolitres of Bourgogne Rouge for a particular house blend, the *courtier*'s role will be to hunt down and offer a suitable parcel.

A newer breed of broker is the one who deals not with the local '*négoce*' but with foreign importers. Such a person need not have as comprehensive a knowledge of all the growers, but will nonetheless have an intimate acquaintance with those whose wines he or she markets. They will work closely with a portfolio of various producers in order to relieve them of the problem of selling their wines. Such brokers have an expanding role now that so many growers are bottling their own wines and cutting out the *négociant* altogether. A broker can help them reach the best foreign markets.

The *courtier* enjoys wide experience and a degree of detachment. Whereas the producers are too close to their problems, and the merchants too distant from them, the broker is able to be objective, and come up with a solution without offending either of the other partners. In an area as infinitely complicated as Burgundy, this role seems assured, for no client can hope to know as much about all the wines of the area as an expert *courtier*. Mutual distrust and suspicion will, no doubt, continue to exist between growers and merchants, but this fact only strengthens the need for the broker.

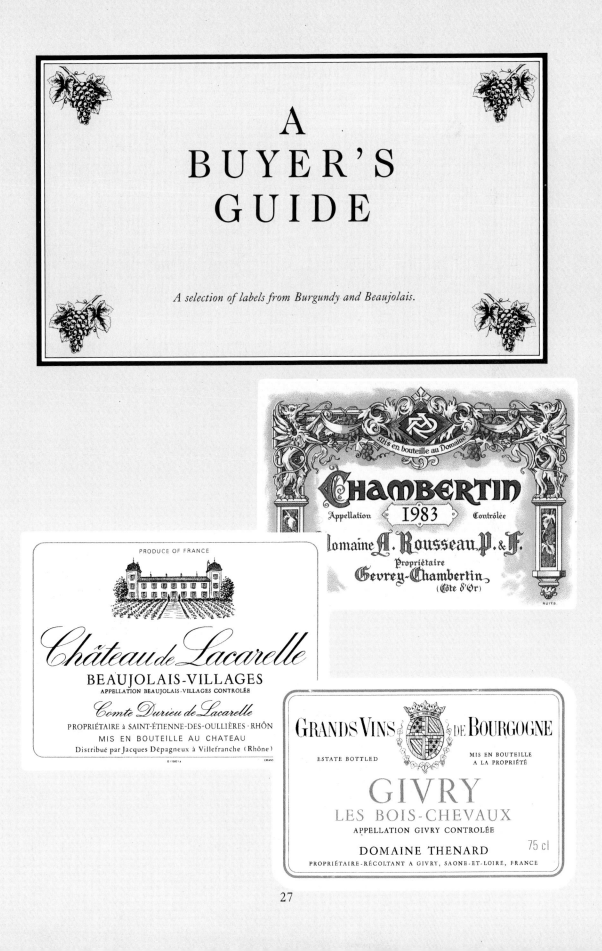

A BUYER'S GUIDE

A selection of labels from Burgundy and Beaujolais.

HOW AND WHERE TO BUY

Fresh food can be bought in a local market by anyone, without fear of serious disappointment. Similarly in the city supermarket you do not usually seek assistance as you shop. No help is required in selecting frozen food or soap powder, and the job of the assistant is simply to take your money, not to give you advice. Buying everyday items is a safe, if unexciting process. With wine, however, the picture is different. Every bottle is more or less of a gamble, and in the case of red burgundy, the stakes are high. It may well pay to seek professional advice.

THREE WAYS TO BUY BURGUNDY

Buying from supermarkets An increasingly significant role is now played by supermarkets, some of which have sophisticated, professionally organized wine departments. Their main role is the sale of everyday wines rather than wines for laying down in a cellar, for *vin de pays* or *vin nouveau* rather than the grander clarets or burgundies. I would be very cautious about buying wines from the Côte d'Or in most supermarkets, unless you are sure they have recently arrived and you know their grower's or merchant's pedigree is impeccable. Beaujolais, on the other hand, should be a safe bet, as it is a robust wine better able to withstand the vicissitudes of supermarket storage and treatment. The prima donna Pinots will respond more favourably when cosseted by a cool cellar rather than subjected to the heat and hassle of a supermarket trolley on a Friday evening.

Buying from a specialist retailer The term 'specialist retailer' can cover a wide variety of operations, from off-licence through wine warehouse and mail-order specialist to the most traditional, oak-panelled breed of merchant in the City of London or Paris. The quality of service and value offered varies wildly. The best way to find out how good any particular specialist retailer is likely to be is to ask questions: if the answers you receive indicate a knowledge of, and commitment to, the wines being sold, then it will be worth your while trying a sample purchase or two. Ignorance and indifference do not inspire confidence. It is, after all, in the retailer's own interest to provide a worthwhile and reliable service to the consumer on whose loyalty he will depend. If you find a merchant able to provide honest advice

based on personal taste, experience and the ability to select the good from the indifferent, then this will be one of the most worthwhile ways of getting good wines at a fair price.

Buying from the grower No wine enthusiast should be discouraged from visiting growers' properties in order to talk and taste with the actual producers. As a formula for bargain-hunting it may prove a disappointment, as comparison with other growers' products is impossible and choice strictly limited, but there is no substitute for the pleasure of drinking a wine when one has had first-hand, personal contact with its birthplace and its maker. Experiences of this sort tend to be particularly rewarding in Burgundy, where small growers with larger-than-life personalities still abound. Distances between *caves* (cellars) are conveniently shorter than in any other of the world's great wine regions.

A caveat would be appropriate, however, for not all growers are as honest or expert as you may think them to be when influenced by the atmosphere of their cellar and a few glasses of their wine. My advice would be to visit growers whose wines you have already found to be exciting, rather than to knock on doors of growers whose names are unfamiliar to you. There is much to be said for having an introduction from a good merchant to one of his growers. You would always be well-advised to make an appointment in advance of arrival, and to remember that you may be overstaying your welcome if you are there for more than one hour. The proprietor of a Burgundy domain is not a salesman, but a wine farmer. As such, if the weather is fine, it is as likely as not that he will wish to be out in his vineyards rather than tied up in his cellar giving a free tasting to a total stranger.

PURCHASING PRINCIPLES

Previous chapters have attempted to identify the problems confronting the producer of red burgundy in the belief that by appreciating the difficulties we will be better prepared for the tricky task of purchasing. We should now consider how best to avoid making unnecessary mistakes, since – Beaujolais aside – any errors made in this field are certain to be expensive ones. I may have given the impression so far that buying burgundy is as dangerous as walking through a minefield. The good news is that there have been a series of major minesweeping expeditions by wine writers, journalists and wine buyers over the last few years, and the situation there is now better than it has been for a long time. It is comparatively easy at present to identify good red burgundy, though less so to obtain it and pay a reasonable price for it. The reason for the improvement is that the growers themselves have scented the incentives and accepted the challenge. No longer enslaved to the *négoce*, their wines have improved enormously.

The bad news is that the consumer will be asked to pay more and more as demand seems likely to continue to far exceed supply. The consumer needs always to bear in mind that Bordeaux, Burgundy's arch rival, produces more than ten times the amount of wine produced by the Côte d'Or and Chablis combined, year by year. Even in the most prolific year, burgundy will always be a scarce commodity. All that the consumer can hope for is that a bottle should justify its price with quality to match. At least it is now actually possible to visit a dozen different producers in the region without any fear of being seriously disappointed. The Côte d'Or should capitalize on its unique strengths and forget about attempts to be more 'commercial'. There are plenty of other areas producing wines suitable for those with a limited budget.

Here are some rules for the prospective buyer.

Rule 1: Taste before you buy Even if you have to pay for the privilege, you would be well advised to taste before buying red burgundy. This is one area in which burgundy presents the consumer with less of a problem than claret, for it is easier to taste when young. It does not need to taste tough and tannic in its youth as a great Médoc does, indeed it is better that it should not do so. Its sensual appeal is direct and requires no translation by intellect. If the wine is unattractive in the barrel, it is not likely to be any more charming in the bottle. Furthermore most vintages do not experience the sort of dull adolescence common in most good Bordeaux wines. (Vintages such as 1976 and 1983 are exceptions for the very reason that they have a tannic structure that is more typical of Bordeaux than Burgundy.)

Even the amateur, therefore, can have considerable confidence when following the evidence of his senses. He or she should learn to recognize real Pinot Noir perfume and the flavour of healthy grapes, and to buy when these are most splendidly present.

Rule 2: Beware bargains There is never enough good burgundy to go round, so no quality producer will ever have to discount his wines. The prospective buyer should learn by comparison what a fair price is for any given appellation and not be tempted to spend less. Bargain-hunting for burgundy generally means looking out for less well-known appellations, or wines from good growers in less fashionable years, or even for wines that have been mis-priced for some reason (burgundy appellations are as confusing for shop assistants as they are for anyone else). But it will be you who spots the bargain; any wine marked as a 'bargain offer' should be treated with suspicion.

Rule 3: Research reliable producers By following the advice your merchant is able to give you, and by assiduous use of one or two of the many detailed guidebooks that exist on Burgundy, you should be able to draw up a list of producers of red burgundy whose credentials are impeccable. Vineyards, vintages and even prices tell you less about quality than the name of a producer. You may still experience disappointing bottles, but this minimizes the risks.

Rule 4: Favour domain-bottled wines While not being an irrefutable truth of Burgundy life, it's still broadly true that a grower has more incentive to make great wines if he bottles and sells under his own name. Many *négociants* are reliable but the same rule holds for them as well: it is usually the wines produced from their own domains that are the best, while their 'village' wines (see pages 30–31) may lack individuality and character, and exhibit instead little more than the house style of the merchant. They will be no cheaper than a grower's wine, indeed they may well be dearer, so there is no saving to be had in putting up with anything less than the best.

To identify genuine domain bottlings look for key phrases on the label such as *Mise en bouteille au domaine*. In Burgundy the terms *château* and *cave* are usually meaningless; better to seek mention of *vigneron*, *viticulteur* or *propriétaire-récoltant*.

To summarize: after the evidence of your senses, the reputation of a good producer is your best guide. It is better than any provided by INAO (*Institut National des Appellations d'Origine*) or the Fraud Squad (*Service des Répressions des Fraudes*), who have nonetheless done much to tighten up control in the region. But no amount of legislation can solve the problem of poor winemaking. By all means learn to understand Burgundy's *Appellation Contrôlée* laws, but make this less of a priority than familiarizing yourself with the names of those producers who can be followed with confidence. There is no substitute for personal experience and knowledge of producers, vineyards and vintages, in that order.

The purpose of a label is to identify a wine for the consumer. But it should also act as some form of guarantee, and the more expensive the wine, the more important the guarantee. The label should therefore protect both the producer and the consumer. Unfortunately the task of ensuring that it does this is next to impossible, for no wine legislation has ever been invented that can give a full guarantee either of authenticity of origin or of quality. Wine appreciation is a subjective matter. No wine can be defined within legally acceptable limits of precision, and wine production is therefore open to opportunities for fraud. The ultimate guarantee of quality is no more or less than the integrity of honest producers whose ambition is to make the best wine they can with the raw materials at their disposal.

Some form of policing, though, is essential. The French *Appellation Contrôlée* laws have been designed to promote and protect the reputation of the best vineyards, and thus to safeguard the heritage of France's most famous national product. Its rules may have been written for the producer's benefit more than the consumer's, but the system does nevertheless help to reduce the opportunities for fraud, and it is a system that has served its original purpose well. It has its shortcomings, but it is true to say that they are outweighed by its advantages. Once again, though, do remember that the words *Appellation Contrôlée* are no guarantee of absolute quality. What they attempt

to guarantee are the following things: area of production, permitted grape varieties, maximum permitted yield and minimum natural alcohol level, as well as the main viticultural practices and vinification techniques. Beyond that, it is up to the grower to do his best, and to the consumer to give or withhold his approval. I have already described the French emphasis on *terroir* – the geology, soils and aspects of individual communes, and it is on this that the laws are founded, rather than, for example, on considerations of sunshine, sugar levels in musts, or levels of alcohol in the finished wine.

The appellations can be divided into five categories: generic appellations for wine produced within a large area (e.g. Bourgogne); specific appellations for wine of a particular district (e.g. Beaujolais, Côte de Beaune-Villages); village appellations (e.g. Gevrey-Chambertin, Nuits-St Georges); Premiers Crus (e.g. Nuits-St Georges 'Les Vaucrains'); and Grands Crus (e.g. Le Chambertin, Corton-Bressandes). Each of these will now be examined in turn.

GENERIC APPELLATIONS

This category, the lowest in the hierarchy by virtue of being the least specific, numbers the following three appellations for red wines:

(a) Bourgogne Grand Ordinaire: an ill-conceived appellation that is used occasionally for blends of Pinot Noir and Gamay with a minimum alcohol con-

This label from the Côte de Beaune village of Volnay indicates that the wine comes from a single Premier Cru vineyard, and that this vineyard is the exclusive property (monopole) of the proprietor.

IL A ÉTÉ TIRÉ 11014 BOUTEILLES ET MAGNUMS DE CETTE CUVÉE

MIS EN BOUTEILLES AU DOMAINE

ESTATE-BOTTLED

•

BOUTEILLE

Nº 11419

VOLNAY Iᴱᴿ CRU — VILLAGE
CLOS DE LA BOUSSE D'OR — VINEYARD

Monopole

APPELLATION VOLNAY CONTROLÉE

1979 — VINTAGE

PRODUCER AND PROPRIETOR

SOCIÉTÉ CIVILE DU DOMAINE DE
LA POUSSE D'OR —
PROPRIÉTAIRE A VOLNAY (COTE-D'OR)
GÉRANT G. POTÈL

FRANCE

e 75 cl

NAME OF MANAGER/WINEMAKER

tent of nine per cent. Even if you find an example nowadays, it is unlikely to be very rewarding.

(b) Bourgogne Passetoutgrain: used for blends of Pinot Noir and Gamay, with the Pinot Noir content at not less than forty per cent and minimum alcohol content of 9.5 per cent. From a good producer, burgundy of this appellation can spring a pleasant surprise at a reasonable price.

(c) Bourgogne: an appellation for any red wine of the region, if made from Pinot Noir (although in certain parts of the Beaujolais district, the Gamay is also allowed). Minimum alcohol content is ten per cent.

SPECIFIC APPELLATIONS

This category narrows the wine's origin down to one of the individual districts of the region, although not to an actual commune. The following appellations are all examples:

Beaujolais and Beaujolais-Villages
Mâcon
Côte de Beaune-Villages
Côte de Nuits-Villages
Bourgogne Hautes Côtes de Beaune
Bourgogne Hautes Côtes de Nuits

VILLAGE APPELLATIONS

The appellation focus now settles on a particular commune or village, and this is the name you will see on the label. You can expect to find more individuality in the character of the wine than for any of the previous categories. You should not, however, expect to find any great wines, for in the Côte d'Or this category will not include wine from the producer's finest vineyards. But you will find yourself paying quite significant sums of money, and you should consider whether or not to pay another ten per cent or so in order to move up from a village wine to one of its best single-estate Premier Cru vineyards. (Wines from non-Premier Cru vineyards may be mentioned on the label in wines of this category, but the quality will probably not be superior to that of the basic village appellation.)

PREMIERS CRUS

This appellation should guarantee you not simply a wine from a single vineyard, but from one of the top sites. Unfortunately the words 'Premier Cru' are not always included on the label, and you should be aware (as described above) that not all single vineyard wines are necessarily Premiers Crus. Most Premiers Crus do draw attention to the fact on their labels, though. Even these can on occasion be a disappointment. This is the category in which the reliable individual domain becomes of paramount significance for the buyer.

GRANDS CRUS

The ultimate appellation in the hierarchy commands a high price and entitles the producer to expect generous rewards. The quality of the vintage and the producer's winemaking will determine whether or not the customer's faith is justified and his money well spent. At this elevated level, the wine dispenses with the name of its village altogether, selling solely on the fame and reputation of the particular vineyard. (The label may also say 'Grand Cru', though again this is optional.) The best wines in Burgundy, therefore, are not named after their villages but their vineyards, confirming the basis of the whole French *Appellation Contrôlée* system on *terroir*.

This label from one of the Beaujolais crus indicates that the wine comes from the vineyard of a single grower in Chénas, but was not bottled at the property. The name of the bottler is therefore shown as well as that of the grower. The vintage will be on a separate neck label.

PRODUCE OF FRANCE

DOMAINE DE CHASSIGNOL — VINEYARD

Chénas

APPELLATION CHENAS CONTRÔLÉE

750 ml

G. FAVRE - Propriétaire à CHENAS (Rhône)

VILLAGE
APPELLATION *CRU*

VINEYARD PROPRIETOR

Mis en bouteille par Jacques DEPAGNEUX - VILLEFRANCHE (Rhône)

création imp. gougenheim lyon

NÉGOCIANT-ÉLEVEUR
AND BOTTLER

VINTAGES

It is notoriously dangerous to generalize about the quality of a vintage in Burgundy, just as it is foolish to make sweeping assessments of the wines of each particular village. There are simply too many exceptions. We have seen how individual growers are the crucial element in the production of red burgundy, and one of the things that distinguishes the great winemaker from the merely competent is his or her ability to adapt vinification techniques to suit the climatic conditions of each year. For the Burgundian weather pattern is far from predictable. The only certainty is that ripening the grapes will be a marginal affair. The vineyards are threatened by spring frosts, poor weather at flowering time, hailstorms of catastrophic ferocity, wet summers and the consequent incidence of rot. Any grower can find himself the victim of extremely trying circumstances, even in a vintage heralded as a major success.

Another problem with generalizing about vintages is that one cannot take into consideration the personal tastes of the reader. Just as commune appellations have differences of style, so too do vintages. Some will find the lighter, elegant years more appealing while others prefer wines with greater power and depth. The age of a wine is a further factor: the Pinot Noir grape can give wonderful soft fruit perfumes when young, or it can be left over a period of years to develop the quite different aromas of well-hung game or the farmyard. In an area where the skill of one individual and the tastes of another are everything, it is inevitably unsatisfactory to make bald, unqualified statements about general quality.

One thing is clear, however, and that is that red Burgundy is a great deal less fortunate with the overall success rate of its vintages than Bordeaux.

1987 At the time of writing, shortly after the harvest, the prospects seem to be for a quite small vintage of correct but probably unspectacular wines.

1986 The large crop brought with it the prospect of a dilution of character in the red wines, as had happened in 1973. In fact it looks as if the better growers have made some excellent wines, superior to those of 1984, though not in the class of the exceptional 1985 wines. They could resemble those of 1979.

Beaujolais also had a big crop but many of the wines seem less precocious than usual. Those who prefer their *crus* (the best wines from the individual, named villages of Fleurie, Morgon, and so on) to have concentration and staying power could be best advised to stay with the better balanced 1985s.

1985 The Côte d'Or wines have all the qualities of a truly great vintage. The fruit is full of charm, with good concentration and a structure that does not allow either the tannin or the acid to predominate. Thus the all-round balance is superb. The vintage appears to be at least as good as 1978. Statistically it must be felt that Burgundy is unlikely to see another vintage of this quality during the decade, so the best wines are well worth buying. They will keep well, though few are likely to last as long as the best 1983s.

The Beaujolais wines are also excellent. No doubt most have been consumed already, but if given a chance, many of the *crus* will keep well for a decade.

1984 This was not a vintage to single out for special praise, but the best wines have elegant fruit, although without much depth. The worst wines are distinctly mean, for the weather was simply too wet and too cool at critical moments. At least there was no rot: the weather in September was too cool for that. Natural alcohol levels were low, and many wines have been overchaptalized as a result. In general it seems wise to drink the wines while they are still young, before the fragile fruit dries out altogether.

In Beaujolais, quality was very modest.

1983 Great red wines were certainly produced this year but they are not for early drinking. The real rewards in store will be for those with the patience to keep them for a decade or more. A strong caveat must be made, unfortunately, for a significant number of wines are flawed by rot, especially in the northern Côte de Nuits, and many of these will seriously disappoint. It was a year which needed careful harvesting and a rigorous selection (*triage*) of healthy grapes. The structure is reminiscent of 1976, but the best wines probably have more weight of fruit.

In Beaujolais, excellent wines were made and the very best will age well for many years.

1982 An uncomfortably large crop meant that much of the wine is dilute, lacking in colour and concentration, but the grapes were fully ripe and generally healthy. Few wines will benefit from prolonged ageing; most are now at, or close to, their peak. Many of the wines are currently attractive in an uncomplicated, easy-drinking way.

In the Beaujolais a similiar lack of concentration made this a year for drinking young.

1981 A minute crop on the Côte d'Or means that few wines from this vintage are available. In general they lack charm, though there are some notable exceptions, where the small crop was healthy and not suffering from the after-effects of hail.

Beaujolais was a good deal more fortunate, though all the wines will now be at, or past, their peak.

1980 Dismissed by at least one prominent *négociant*, the reputation of this vintage has required a good deal of rehabilitation. On the Côte de Nuits it fully deserves it, for many growers have produced wines at least as good as their 1979 offerings. The Côte de Beaune was less satisfactory, even for white wines, which is most unusual.

It was a relatively weak vintage in Beaujolais, and by now all the wines should have been drunk.

1979 A satisfactory vintage but with few great wines. The crop was large and the acidity too low to make for longevity. Most wines are at their peak after six years in bottle.

1978 A very good, even great vintage, with wines of excellent healthy fruit, well-balanced by acidity and tannin. The style of each village came through clearly in the right hands and the wines should age very well.

1977 The poorest vintage of the decade discussed here. Remaining wines should not be kept long, since there will be little to recommend them when their tenuous fruit has dried out.

1976 An untypical Burgundy vintage, built more in the style of Bordeaux, with quite massive tannin in some cases. The question mark that hangs over many wines is whether there is enough fruit to balance that tannin as it softens over the years. Some are looking distinctly unbalanced in this respect and further ageing may only accentuate the problem. Others still require patience and the rewards could be magnifi-

cent for the best of them. The worst are characterized by dry tannin and fading fruit. Elegance is not a feature of the wines of this vintage.

Here are some other post-war vintages worth looking out for:

1972 Underrated when very young, the high acidity of this vintage often obscured its potential balance: this is proving a fine year for the red wines of the Côte d'Or.

1971 Overripeness frequently caused imbalance in the wines of this vintage but, balanced or not, there are some rich and voluptuous treats to be found here.

1969 A great vintage of wines with marvellous flavour and perfect balance.

1966 The best wines had great depth and have only recently reached full maturity.

1959 Rich and powerful wines from a very warm year.

1955 Wines of breed and balance that have aged well.

1953 Supremely graceful wines that have lasted just as well as more powerful ones.

1949 A great vintage that combined power with elegance.

1947 Exotic wines packed with ripe fruit and plenty of alcoholic staying power.

The glass is now generally used for tasting, but the tastevin *remains the traditional tool of the Burgundian winetaster.*

PRICE STRUCTURE

Value for money in relation to red burgundy has little to do with a particular wine's being cheap. A wine that is unpleasant to drink is bad value at any price. Conversely, an expensive wine may represent excellent value if it offers the drinker exceptional pleasure. A good quality/price ratio within each of the categories discussed below is what the burgundy enthusiast should look for.

INEXPENSIVE BURGUNDY
(PRICE RANGE £3.00 – £5.00)

No good or genuine burgundy will ever find itself in the 'Bargain Basement', for this is a region of low yields and high demand from consumers. But happily there are still relatively inexpensive wines that are fair representatives of Burgundy. Names to look for within this category are the generic appellations Bourgogne Rouge and Bourgogne Passetoutgrain, ordinary Beaujolais and Beaujolais-Villages, some Mâcon Rouge and the less expensive wines of the Hautes Côtes. The appellation Bourgogne Grande Ordinaire is a peculiar one: the concept of being simultaneously 'great' and 'ordinary' is one that surely carries little credibility outside France! It is an illustration of the way that some legislation seems to exist for the benefit of the producer rather than the consumer, carrying as it does the implication that Burgundy is incapable of producing any wine that is mediocre, while it is well-known that the opposite is true. The 'ordinaire' part of the title is the part that describes the wine most accurately: as an appellation it has little future. Cheap, 'generic' Nuits-St Georges is already a thing of the past, fortunately, for it was far more likely to be a fraud than a bargain. Any apparently knowledgeable sales talk about bargains based on declassified surplus production should be treated with extreme suspicion, for Burgundy is an area where excess production is negligible. Most of the time there is not enough wine, and that is precisely why prices here start at a relatively high level, certainly when compared to Bordeaux.

The Bourgogne Rouge appellation is confusing, as the style can vary considerably, depending on whether the wine comes from the north or the south of the region. The Bourgogne Rouge of a grower in Volnay will be made from Pinot Noir grapes, while that of a grower in Fleurie will be made entirely from the Gamay grape. The rules allow for both. Given this anomalous situation, you should make every effort to discover the true origin of a Bourgogne Rouge before buying, and check in particular if the grower's or merchant's address is in Beaujolais. If it is, you will probably be buying Beaujolais, and it may not be very good. Some Côte d'Or Bourgogne Rouge wines are excellent value for money, though. It is an absurd situation, and this is another instance where the rules are clearly to blame.

Bourgogne Passetoutgrain is a blend of both of the region's red grape varieties to a maximum of two-thirds Gamay and a minimum of one-third Pinot Noir. If you are lucky, the proportion of Pinot Noir may be considerably higher, especially in a large vintage like 1982. From a keen, small grower, both this appellation and Bourgogne Rouge wines can indeed be excellent value. He or she may have some old, well-sited vines that may just miss out on their village appellation by being on the wrong side of the path. Alternatively there may be some wine from young vines on a particularly good site which are not entitled to the top appellation because of their youth, but which nonetheless bear the hallmarks of the *terroir* even if they lack something in real concentration. Such wines may offer real value for money. But both Bourgogne Rouge and Bourgogne Passetoutgrain can also be characterless wines, whether from large commercial houses, or from prestigious growers whose hearts are in their Grands Crus rather than their basic appellation wines (which will in any case command an inflated price based on the fame of that producer). The best advice here, as usual, is to follow a producer whose style you have learnt to trust and enjoy, and ask to try his cheapest wines.

Wines from villages outside the main Côte d'Or area such as Irancy or Dezize-lès-Maranges (see page 39 and page 60) and from fringe areas like the Hautes Côtes (see pages 60-61), are a reasonable buy in good vintages. In weak, wet years they can be decidedly disappointing. As for basic Beaujolais, most of the best wine is now sold as Beaujolais Nouveau, and because this market is so competitive, it is usually easy to find drinkable wines at a relatively low price, expecially in a good vintage.

MEDIUM-PRICED BURGUNDY
(PRICE RANGE £5.00–£12.00)

If you want wines of real personality from the Côte d'Or, you should look for something from an individual village or vineyard, choosing, if possible, from a producer whose style you like and whose reputation is trustworthy. It is not necessary to go for well-known villages; in fact there is much to be said for avoiding them. Remember that even poor wine will sell quite easily if it is called Gevrey-Chambertin or Nuits-St Georges, but if a wine is called St Aubin or Monthelie, it will be trying to impress you with its quality and the value that it offers compared with a more famous neighbour. One pays for smart labels on wine bottles as on clothes or cars.

It is still just possible at the time of writing to procure really individual fine red burgundy from single vineyards of good domains without spending more than about £10 per bottle. These *may* be plain 'village' appellation wines from any of the most famous communes, such as Gevrey or Volnay, but a happier hunting ground is to be found in the best sites of the second-rank villages. It is thus worth searching out the best wines from places such as Santenay (e.g. La Comme), St Aubin (e.g. La Chatenière), Auxey-Duresses, Monthelie, and Pernand-Vergelesses. All of these are from the Côte de Beaune. Fame and consequent high prices have caught up with just about all the communes of the Côte de Nuits, with the exception of Fixin and Marsannay.

Sadly, the better-value villages often choose, even nowadays, to sell under the generic name of Côte de Beaune-Villages or Côte de Nuits-Villages, forsaking the greater individuality they are entitled to in favour of a more ready commercial identity. The results are often characterless blends.

Nearly all the wines of the Côte Chalonnaise should fit comfortably into this price bracket, and some of them are very good. None will bear comparison with the best of the Côte d'Or, but many will compare favourably, in both price and quality, with the lesser village reds of the Côte d'Or. Mercurey and Givry in particular should not disappoint.

Beaujolais has much to offer in this range, for while it does not produce any wines than can be called great, it is equally true that its best wines are never exorbitantly priced, and can be very good. Those that command particular attention are the better Beaujolais-Villages wines and the individual *crus* (see page 70ff). Of these, Fleurie is the most fashionable and is therefore likely to be least good value. The canny buyer will do better to look for wine from Morgon or Chénas. Unfortunately the fine distinctions between the wines of the different villages often become blurred in the hands of the larger *négociants* and those whose centres of operation are outside the region in Beaune, for example. So look for a Beaujolais address as well as a Beaujolais name on the bottle.

LUXURY BURGUNDY
(PRICE RANGE £12.00 UPWARDS)

Perhaps the first piece of advice when dealing with this category is to try and forget about the price. In the case of red burgundy, paying a high price is no guarantee of high quality. It is all too often true that expensive burgundy proves disappointing.

In this category, we can restrict our selections to the wines of the Côte de Nuits and, to a lesser extent, the Côte de Beaune. It is generally true to say that in the communes of the Côte d'Or the named vineyard sites are worth the extra price they command. For ten or fifteen per cent more money it is possible to move from a village wine to a Premier Cru. This will provide an extra dimension of flavour in the wine at an extra cost of perhaps £1.00 or 10 francs per bottle, and this threshold should deter no serious burgundy enthusiast. The next move up, from Premier Cru to Grand Cru, may pose more of a strain on the budget: here one moves into an area for the very rich or genuinely obsessed. Grands Crus are, objectively speaking, worth more than Premiers, but exactly how much more is a consideration for the individual buyer. The genuine rarity of these wines inevitably pushes their prices to the levels of those commanded by the 'first growths' of Bordeaux, yet a vineyard like Richebourg may only produce five per cent of the quantity produced by Château Lafite-Rothschild. In this perspective, Grand Cru burgundies can be seen to be good value.

To sum up, there are two approaches one might take to buying burgundy, depending on the width of one's wallet. Buy the best if money is no object, looking for Grands Crus and the best Premiers Crus from the best growers in the best villages. If your resources are limited, though, seek out wines from the less well-known villages; you will be paying less for the label and patronizing producers who have something to prove. Growers in Gevrey may be blasé about sales and bored by strangers ringing their doorbells, but their counterparts in Pernand-Vergelesses are more likely to be flattered by serious interest in Paris or London. That is the kind of situation that spells good value, and one should take such opportunities while they remain.

THROUGH
THE
VINEYARDS

*Sunlight filters through the misty and indistinct winter landscape of a
Burgundian village. Tasks such as pruning and repairing equipment
ensure that there is never any shortage of work for the vigneron.*

The rest of the book takes the reader on a guided tour through the different districts of Burgundy, village by village, from north to south. The importance and the style of the wines of each village will be assessed, its principal vineyard sites identified and described and a selective list of the best producers given. These lists make no claim to be up-to-date or fully comprehensive, because the situation changes fast, as more or less capable and enthusiastic sons succeed their fathers. My intention is that these should be practical and personal lists of producers in which I have full confidence. Asterisks indicate producers I consider to have achieved particular winemaking excellence.

A sea of sunbathing vineyards surround this little hamlet on the road from St Amour to Juliénas, two of the best villages in the Beaujolais district. Nowhere else in the world makes such successful wine from the Gamay grape.

THE YONNE

In terms of the production of red burgundy, the vineyards of the Yonne (the home of Chablis) are of little significance. They lie over one hundred kilometres northwest of the Côte d'Or, near the town of Auxerre. But in a viticultural sense, if the Gamay wines of the Beaujolais are allowed to be classified as burgundy, then that honour cannot be denied the Pinot Noir wines of the Yonne. They are lacking in depth and power for the vineyards are much further north and are grown on the lighter Kimmeridgian clays responsible for fine Chablis. In recent years, though, the wines of Irancy and Coulanges-la-Vineuse have experienced a growth in popularity and expansion has consequently taken place. In addition to the Pinot Noir, a local variety called the César is also grown – a grape that is presumed to date from the arrival of Caesar's legions here in the first century BC. This variety gives colour, tannin and acidity, while the very light Pinot Noir produced on this soil contributes finesse. Another red grape variety, the Tressot, is also permitted here. It is even more obscure, however, and has now almost vanished altogether, not having responded well to grafting in the post-phylloxera era. It is a safe assumption that its quality is modest enough to discourage perseverance. When planted, both these rare grapes are vinified together with the predominant Pinot Noir.

Irancy has had its own AC since 1976. Elsewhere the red wine must be classified as Bourgogne Rouge, though wines from Coulanges-la-Vineuse are permitted to make mention of the fact on the label.

Good Yonne producers	
Léon Bienvenue, Irancy	André Martin,
Bernard Cantin, Irancy	Coulanges-la-Vineuse
Robert Colinot, Irancy	Jean Podor, Irancy
Roger Delaloge, Irancy	Luc Sorin, Irancy
Raymond Dupuis,	
Coulanges-la-Vineuse	

The houses of Irancy, near Auxerre, lie huddled together at the foot of a sweeping amphitheatre of vineyards. Although the vineyards of the Yonne are famous for Chablis, red wine has been made here for two thousand years.

THE CÔTE DE NUITS

THE CÔTE D'OR

The fame and reputation of Burgundy rests primarily on this stretch of vineyards, subdivided into the Côte de Nuits and the Côte de Beaune. The former runs from Chenôve, on the outskirts of Dijon, southwards as far as Corgoloin. The latter then takes over and stretches from Ladoix down through Santenay to Sampigny-lès-Maranges in the department of Saône-et-Loire.

In general, it is said that the wines of the Côte de Beaune are relatively precocious, full of bouquet and elegance, while those of the Côte de Nuits have more power and flavour – if given time, for they are wines of greater longevity. In earlier times Burgundians spoke of the *vins de primeur* of the Côte de Beaune and the *vins de garde* of the Côte de Nuits, meaning that the former required four to five years to reach maturity, while the latter would need twelve to fifteen years. This difference is based on contrasts in the soil and exposure of the two Côtes. It is, though, not difficult to find exceptions to the rule.

An illustration of the complications of *terroir* in this region is the fact that fifty-nine separate soil types can be differentiated within the Côte de Nuits. Within the commune of Nuits-St Georges alone, over fifty different *climats* can be identified in just a hundred hectares. (The word *climat* signifies a single vineyard site understood in terms of the combination of soil characteristics and exposure it possesses.)

MARSANNAY-LA-CÔTE

North of this village the vineyards have been almost wiped out by the urban sprawl of Dijon (though in Chenôve, the Clos du Roy and Clos du Chapitre still produce a small amount of respectable wine). Marsannay is therefore the most northerly commune in France's northernmost fine red wine area and, perhaps as a consequence, it has had to be somewhat adaptable in order to survive.

Until the end of the eighteenth century it had a fine reputation for its Pinot Noir. Thereafter, as Dijon grew larger, its role became that of a supplier of ordinary red wines to quench the thirsts of the large population at whose doorstep it lay. (We should remember that communications in those days were less sophisticated than they are now, and villages such as this could hardly expect to live off any international reputation.) In order to meet requirements, the Gamay, with its generous yields of quick maturing wine, took over the vineyards until, by the end of the nineteenth century, not a Pinot vine was to be found there. However, after the First World War, the Gamay encountered severe competition from cheaper imports of full-bodied wine from the Midi and Algeria. The *vignerons* of Marsannay, following the example of leading grower Joseph Clair, switched back to the Pinot Noir again, this time to create a rosé that is one of the best in France. A small cooperative was established in 1929 and Marsannay rapidly established a unique reputation.

The Domaine Clair-Daü is a major producer of this Rosé de Marsannay. The red wine from vineyards on the slope can also be excellent in good vintages, and is worthy of the appellation that has recently been granted to the village, after years of campaigning by the growers. Marsannay, in fact, is the only Burgundian appellation that can be applied to red, white and rosé wines.

Good Marsannay producers	
André Bart	Domaine Clair-Daü*
René Bouvier	Jean Fournier*
Philippe Charlopin-Parizot*	Huguenot Père & Fils
Bruno Clair	Charles Quillardet

COUCHEY

This commune now shares the appellation of Marsannay. Its best vineyard site, Champs-Perdrix, is a *climat* that falls partly in Fixin, and is as propitiously situated as some Côte de Nuits Premiers Crus. At least the latest legislation now allows it a higher status than that of the humble Bourgogne Rouge it previously had to endure.

Good Couchey producers	
Clemancey Frères	Jean Tardy
Sirugue Père & Fils	

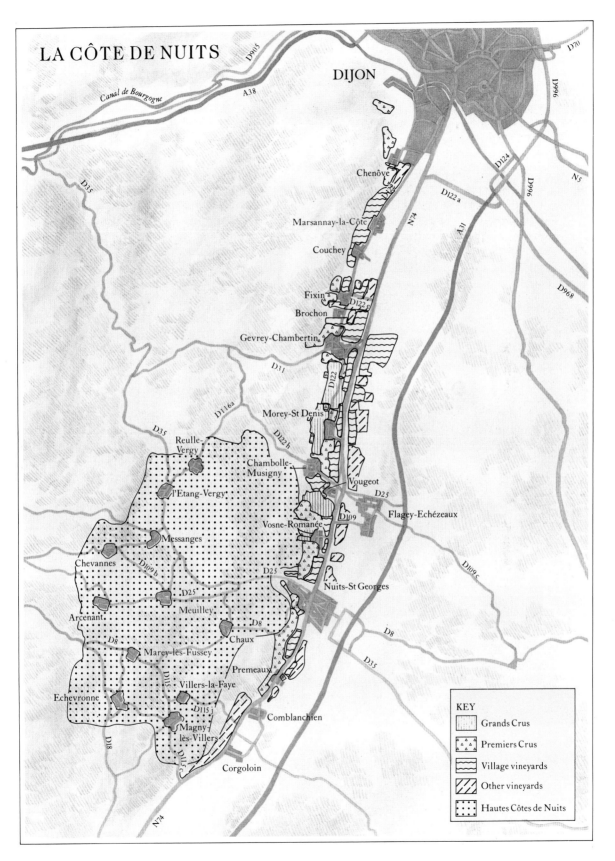

LA CÔTE DE NUITS

Canal de Bourgogne

DIJON

Chenôve

Marsannay-la-Côte

Couchey

Fixin

Brochon

Gevrey-Chambertin

Morey-St Denis

Reulle-Vergy

Chambolle-Musigny

l'Etang-Vergy

Vougeot

Flagey-Echézeaux

Vosne-Romanée

Messanges

Chevannes

Nuits-St Georges

Arcenant

Meuilley

Chaux

Marey-lès-Fussey

Premeaux

Villers-la-Faye

Echevronne

Comblanchien

Magny-lès-Villers

Corgoloin

KEY

Grands Crus

Premiers Crus

Village vineyards

Other vineyards

Hautes Côtes de Nuits

FIXIN

Fixin growers have often found it easier to sell their wines under the generic banner of Côte de Nuits-Villages (see page 49), and the village or generic appellations are interchangeable within the commune – a situation not permitted in the other villages entitled to the Côte de Nuits appellation, such as Corgoloin or Comblanchien.

Fixin's red wines are characterized by solidity rather than finesse. They possess vinosity, deep colour, a bouquet that reveals itself with time, and ample tannin to allow for longevity. A favourable microclimate leaves it comparatively untouched by the excesses of Burgundian weather and there has

been hardly a serious hailstorm in living memory. Fixin remains relatively unknown, hence its frequent decision to sell under the more widely recognized appellation of Côte de Nuits-Villages. Yet its Premiers Crus easily match the quality of some of Gevrey's Premiers Crus, and it is worth recalling that in 1855 the price of Clos de la Perrière matched that of Chambertin. Nowadays there is a lot of argument as to whether the Clos de la Perrière or the Clos du Chapitre makes the finest red wine. Both lie on steep gradients and possess similar soils: a rich brown limestone mix with plenty of pebbles. By contrast, Les Hervelets and Les Arvelets are on a very gentle slope of sandy limestone, with a thin topsoil, giving wines of a markedly lighter style, with more finesse and less power. Aux Cheusots is virtually flat, and the wine from its Clos Napoléon is also lighter than that of adjacent Clos du Chapitre.

Premiers Crus	
Les Arvelets	Les Hervelets
Aux Cheusots	Les Meix-Bas
(including Clos Napoléon)	Clos de la Perrière
Clos du Chapitre	

Good Fixin producers	
André Bart	Pierre Gelin*
Vincent & Denis Berthaut	Philippe Joliet*
Bruno Clair	Domaine Mongeard-Mugneret

GEVREY-CHAMBERTIN

Gevrey, from its 592 hectares of vineyards, produces more wine than any other commune on the Côte d'Or, despite having a smaller vineyard area than Beaune. This fact alone should be enough to make the buyer exercise caution, for overproduction is the great enemy of high quality. It will come as no surprise therefore to find that the quality of much basic village Gevrey leaves a good deal to be desired. However, this is a commune that boasts no less than nine Grands Crus and twenty-six Premiers Crus, some of which, notably Le Clos St-Jacques, make wine of comparable stature to the Grands Crus.

This is the first of the undeniably great communes that one reaches on the way south from Dijon. Just as Puligny has gained world fame by virtue of its association with Le Montrachet, so Gevrey owes its glory principally to the vineyard of Le Chambertin. Mon-

Grape pickers and Fixin's church bathed in late afternoon sunshine. Wines from here are known more for solidity than finesse, but elegance and power can also be present in them.

trachet lays claim to be the greatest dry white wine in the world, and Chambertin makes similar claims as a red wine, though the accolade is hotly contested even within the region. There is no doubt, though, that at its best Chambertin is a wine that epitomizes great red burgundy.

In general, the wines of Gevrey are deeply coloured, tough and well able to support plenty of bottle ageing. Indeed they often need bottle ageing, and are unattractive if drunk young. Other communes on the Côte de Nuits may produce wines that are more subtle, but few can boast wines that are so complete. Various celebrated local authors have acknowledged this. Camille Rodier has written of Chambertin that it "possesses in the highest degree all the qualities that characterize a perfect wine — body, colour, bouquet and finesse." Gaston Roupnel, who is buried in Gevrey, described Chambertin as being as firm and full-bodied as a Corton, as delicate as Musigny, as velvety as a Romanée and as perfumed as a Clos de Vougeot. It is a wine that demands patience, for by normal Côte d'Or standards it can seem remarkably harsh when young.

All the Grands Crus are situated on a base of sandy limestone, on sloping ground that reaches up to 300 metres in altitude. The topsoil is composed of brown chalky soil with a variable amount of clay and plenty of pebbles. In some *crus*, notably Griotte- and Chapelle-Chambertin, the soil is thin and the rock is occasionally exposed. Mazoyères-Chambertin lies on gravel close to the rock, while Latricières- and Ruchottes-Chambertin are on oolitic limestone. The best Premiers Crus – Le Clos St Jacques, Les Varoilles and Les Cazetiers are at the same altitude as Le Chambertin, but are less well-protected by the forest on the top of the hill and more exposed to the cold winds that blow down the Combe de Lavaux. This is a commune where it is usually well worth paying extra for a Premier Cru: they are significantly better than the 'village' wines and in some instances, especially that of the Clos St Jacques, can stand up to a Chambertin Grand Cru without a hint of inferiority. The price fetched by Armand Rousseau's wine clearly substantiates this claim.

Lower down the hill, the village appellation extends much further than normal out on to the flatter land of the plain, even across the Route Nationale and on towards the railway line. The land here, although lacking a slope to provide it with drainage, benefits from plenty of gravel, so it is probable that any dull Gevrey-Chambertin wines are the result of excessive yields or poor winemaking.

Good Gevrey-Chambertin producers	
Domaine Drouhin	Bernard Maume
Domaine Drouhin-Laroze	Joseph Roty
Jean-Claude Fourrier	Armand Rousseau*
Philippe Leclerc	Louis Trapet
Henri Magnien	Domaine des Varoilles

MOREY-SAINT DENIS

Morey, with just over 100 hectares to its name, seems to have suffered in marketing terms by falling between the two glamorous villages of Gevrey and Chambolle. It is smaller and less well-known than either. The quality of its soil and vineyards, though, matches that of its neighbours.

It boasts five Grands Crus, and there are some particularly fine Premiers Crus amongst its total of twenty. Stylistically as well as geographically they lie between Gevrey and Chambolle, combining the strength of the former with the finesse of the latter. As with Gevrey, Aloxe, Puligny and others, Morey's lengthened name is the result of the village borrowing the fame of one of its finest vineyards, the Clos St Denis. The big merchants have usually found it simpler to bend the rules and sell much of Morey's village wine either as Gevrey-Chambertin or Chambolle-Musigny. Thus it has remained a bit of an underdog until recently, when it has at last been discovered and revealed to the world as a fine *cru* at a reasonable price. As a result Morey is beginning to enjoy the self-confidence needed to commercialize its wines as effectively as its neighbours. Bargain-hunters will soon have to look elsewhere!

GEVREY-CHAMBERTIN	
Grands Crus	**Premiers Crus**
Chambertin	Clos St Jacques
Chambertin-Clos de Bèze	Les Varoilles (or
Chapelle-Chambertin	Véroilles)
Charmes-Chambertin	Cazetiers
Griotte-Chambertin	Champeaux
Latricières-Chambertin	Combe aux Moines
Mazis-Chambertin	Combottes
Ruchottes-Chambertin	Lavaux-St Jacques

The first two Grands Crus should be in a class of their own, while all should be memorable wines. Of the Premiers Crus, the first two vineyards can match the quality of many of the Grands Crus.

Geologically Morey's slope is similar to the adjacent Gevrey, with a sandy limestone underlay for the Grands Crus. Calcareous soil in both the Clos de Tart and the Morey part of the Bonnes Mares *climat* gives a fairly lean and austere style to these wines; both age well. The Clos de la Roche and Clos St Denis benefit from well-sheltered locations and make wines that are similar in character to Chambertin, though without its aggressivity.

MOREY-SAINT DENIS	
Grands Crus	**Top Premiers Crus**
Bonnes Mares	Clos de la Bussière
Clos des Lambrays	Aux Charmes
Clos de la Roche	Clos des Ormes
Clos St Denis	Les Ruchots
Clos de Tart	Clos des Sorbés

Good Morey-St Denis producers	
Domaine Arlaud Père & Fils	Georges Lignier*
Domaine Dujac*	Domaine Ponsot
Domaine des Lambrays	J. Truchot-Martin

CHAMBOLLE-MUSIGNY

Chambolle has a fine reputation in spite of being relatively small. It has only 223 hectares of vineyard, and is well below half the size of Gevrey, with whose wines its own contrast clearly. Chambolle's wines are characterized by extreme delicacy and are for those who appreciate a fine, lingering perfume, and great subtlety of flavour. The greatest wine here, Le

CHAMBOLLE-MUSIGNY	
Grands Crus	**Top Premiers Crus**
Bonnes Mares	Les Amoureuses
Le Musigny	Les Charmes

Good Chambolle-Musigny producers	
Bernard Amiot	Jacques-Frédéric Mugnier
Gaston Barthod-Noëllat	Georges Roumier
Domaine Clair-Daü	Bernard Serveau
Alain Hudelot-Noëllat	Domaine Comte Georges
Daniel Moine-Hudelot	de Vogüé

Musigny, is the antithesis of Le Chambertin: silk as opposed to steel. But any apparent lightness of style should not deceive one into thinking that the wines lack longevity, for their fine balance means that they keep extremely well. The strength of the wine is masked by its seductive delicacy.

The clue to its character lies in the soil, which is predominantly limestone rather than clay. The steep slope of Le Musigny itself, squeezed below the crest of the hill, has white oolite at the top and some red clay to add richness. (A very small amount of white Le Musigny is made.) The other Grand Cru in Chambolle is Bonnes Mares (most – nearly fourteen hectares – of this vineyard lies in Chambolle, while a smaller part lies in Morey). The wines produced here are more powerful, though not as hard and Chambertin-like as those that the Morey segment produces. The top Premiers Crus are well-known: Les Amoureuses and Les Charmes, of which the former is thought more elegant, perhaps due to its lying further up the hill and nearer Le Musigny itself. The village is the home of the famous estate of the Comte de Vogüé which controls around seventy per cent of the production of Musigny.

VOUGEOT

Vougeot, the smallest commune on the Côte d'Or, is Burgundy in microcosm. Notorious for the variable quality of its wines, particularly the Grand Cru Clos de Vougeot, it is a perfect illustration of the problems of the region. The fifty hectares of the Clos de Vougeot itself, which forms over eighty per cent of the commune's vineyard area, is split between some seventy-seven or so proprietors. Added to this is the fact that the Clos itself is geologically diverse – an amalgamation of many disparate *climats* – some of which are suited for the production of a wine worthy of its Grand Cru status while the others very definitely are not. It is only the sturdy wall that surrounds it which has protected its artificial integrity for so long. Were this *clos* a *monopole* (i.e. in the exclusive ownership of one proprietor, as is often the case with a *clos*), he or she would make a selection of the best wine and declassify the rest. Unfortunately, the ownership problems of Burgundy exclude this possibility and we are left with the frustrating situation that a Grand Cru appellation is one of the least reliable in the area.

The soils within the Clos can be broadly put into three categories. The highest part is regarded as the best. It rests on calcareous oolite with a clay/gravel

*Storm clouds loom over the Grand Cru vineyards and
the Château of the Clos de Vougeot. Over seventy
different proprietors share the fifty hectares of this appellation.*

admixture providing the chalky brown soil emi-
nently suitable for great wine. By contrast, the lowest
part has an alluvial deposit, with deep, poorly
drained soil that is nothing like so favourable. (In
fact the Clos de Vougeot runs down the slope as far as
the Route Nationale and is the only Grand Cru
vineyard that lies at an altitude of less than 250
metres (820 feet) above sea level.) The middle section is composed of soft limestone and clay, better
drained because of the gravel mixed in with it.

It is said that the monks of Cîteaux, who originally
enclosed the vineyard, were able to produce three
different wines from the Clos: La Cuvée des Papes,
La Cuvée des Rois, and La Cuvée des Moines. The
popes and kings enjoyed a true Grand Cru, while the
monks made do with the more ordinary wine, from
today's roadside. Another possibility is that the winemaking brothers realized the potential of the whole
vineyard by intelligent blending. What remains
incontestable is the lack of uniformity about the
wines of the Clos de Vougeot today, and here, especially, the grower's name will be your best guide.

Another important distinction to remember is
between the Clos de Vougeot and a simple village
Vougeot. The village wine can be decent, but is
generally inferior to a village Chambolle-Musigny.
There are also three Premiers Crus for red wine and
a small amount of rarely seen Vougeot and Vougeot
Premier Cru Blanc.

VOUGEOT	
Grand Cru	**Premiers Crus**
Clos de Vougeot	Le Clos de la Perrière
	Les Cras
	Les Petits Vougeot

Good Vougeot producers	
Domaine Bertagna	Jean Gros*
Georges Clerget	Domaine Mongeard-
Joseph Drouhin*	Mugneret*
Domaine Drouhin-Laroze	Domaine Daniel Rion

VOSNE-ROMANÉE AND FLAGEY-ECHÉZEAUX

The wines of Flagey-Echézeaux, a commune lying east of the Route Nationale, may be conveniently bracketed with those of Vosne-Romanée, since Flagey has no village appellation of its own. Its Grands Crus are those of Echézeaux and Grands Echézeaux, while its lesser wines are sold as Vosne-Romanée. Of the Grands Crus, Echézeaux reaches the exceptional altitude of 360 metres, and even at this height the soil here is still relatively rich and deep. The gradient is significantly more severe than that of the Grands Echézeaux below it, and there should be a detectable difference in the character of the two *crus*, the lighter elegance of the Echézeaux contrasting with the deeper flavour and staying power of the Grands Echézeaux. In practice, the winemaking style of the grower is of more importance than the difference in soils.

Vosne-Romanée itself is the jewel in the Côte de Nuits crown. "There are no common wines in Vosne" it is said. Certainly with such vineyards there *should* be none, but as always in Burgundy there are disappointing wines that do not realize their potential. Much of the village's fame reflects the fact that this is the home of the Domaine de la Romanée-Conti, responsible for the great *monopoles* of Romanée-Conti and La Tâche, but also for exquisite Echézeaux, Grands Echézeaux, Romanée-St Vivant and Richebourg. Eighty per cent of its wines are exported. No expense is spared in the search for quality and the wines have an excellent capacity for ageing. The Echézeaux may be somewhat lighter and less tannic than the Grands Echézeaux, but it has a penetrating perfume and great elegance. The Richebourg is characterized by great depth and richness, while La Tâche and the Romanée-Conti itself can somehow transcend the realm of mere wine, transforming themselves into an indescribable elixir of ethereal richness and balance, masculine and feminine, a fusion of power and elegance. These wines reflect the grape and its *terroir* to perfection. Such is the quality of ripe fruit from the old vines that one can scarcely detect the influence of new wood on the overall structure and complexity of the wines. The picture is marred only by the price. Regrettably, worldwide demand means that the price of the Domaine's wines seems ridiculous to all but millionaires.

It goes without saying that the soils here are admirably suited to the production of great wine, the finest

*A broad expanse of undulating vineyard land in Vosne-Romanée, famed for many of
Burgundy's finest red wines. The reddish soils are a combination of clay and limestone.*

The most expensive plot of land in Burgundy is the Romanée-Conti vineyard in Vosne-Romanée.

VOSNE-ROMANÉE AND FLAGEY-ECHÉZEAUX	
Grand Crus	**Premiers Crus**
La Romanée	Les Beaumonts
Romanée-Conti	Les Brûlées
Romanée-St Vivant	La Grande Rue
Richebourg	Aux Malconsorts
La Tâche	Les Suchots
Echézeaux	
Grands Echézeaux	

Good Vosne-Romanée and Flagey-Echézeaux producers	
Robert Arnoux	Domaine
Jean Grivot	Mongeard-Mugneret*
Jean Gros	Domaine de la
Henri Jayer*	Romanée-Conti*
Domaine Lamarche	Robert Sirugue

NUITS-SAINT GEORGES

lying (as usual) in the middle part of the slope, with a well-drained combination of limestone, clay and pebbles. Romanée-Conti is marked by brown chalky soil with iron and clay, while Romanée-St Vivant has deeper clay and plenty of limestone. La Tâche lies on less of a slope, but the presence of the decomposed rock and small pebbles facilitates its drainage. Old vines on the best sites allow a small handful of skilful growers to make wines of comparable quality to those of the Domaine de la Romanée-Conti. It is not hard to understand why the wines of Vosne have been described as bottled velvet. But with almost 100 hectares of basic village appellation, care must be exercised at the lower end of the scale, for there *are* moderate wines to be found here, in spite of claims to the contrary. At their best, the village wines should elegantly combine flavours of fruit and spice.

While not denying the importance of the Domaine de la Romanée-Conti, its fame should not be allowed to dwarf the reputation of some of the other producers here who are capable of producing equally great wines from these exceptional sites. No better illustration of this could be found than Henri Jayer, an example of all that is best in the small Burgundian domain. Conscientious and thorough in both the vineyard and the cellar, he combines the sagacity of long experience and inherited tradition with the instinct, flair and intuitive skills of a natural genius.

The more famous the name of a wine village, the more the buyer should be on his guard when purchasing a bottle of wine that bears that name. Exercise, therefore, more caution when buying Gevrey or Nuits than Morey or Chambolle. Nuits-St Georges has a larger vineyard area than even Gevrey has, and by virtue of its evocative name and the size of its production, it can claim to be Burgundy's best known and loved appellation. But while Gevrey-Chambertin basks in the reflected glory of its Grands Crus, Nuits-St Georges has none to offer. It does, though, have some impressive potential among its twenty-seven Premiers Crus, and has incorporated into its name that of one of its two best vineyards. There may be local political reasons why Nuits has no Grands Crus, but the reason should be that its wines are incapable of scaling the heights achieved by the best wines of Gevrey and Vosne. (This is largely true, but one can't help noting that many Nuits Premiers Crus are superior to many wines entitled to the Grand Cru Clos de Vougeot.) Nuits wines have a consistency of character, a pleasing robustness on the palate coupled with a fragrance of aroma which can make them thoroughly satisfactory, if ultimately less magnificent than some of the wines from its northern neighbours.

The valley of the Meuzin effectively splits the vineyard into two halves, the northern half stretching up to Vosne, and the southern half running into the commune of Premeaux (whose wines are sold under the Nuits appellation). The two main sectors are marked by a perceptible difference of style. In the northern part, the wines have fragrance and a subtle elegance that reminds one of Vosne. The soils get progressively heavier, and the wines correspondingly more robust, as the vines get nearer Nuits itself. Thus wines from Les Damodes, La Richemone and part of Aux Chaignots are marked by perfume, while those of Les Vaucrains and Les St Georges are distinguished by flavour and body. The Premiers Crus on the Vosne side lie at a higher altitude than those to the south and in Premeaux, where they run adjacent to the Route Nationale. But there are wines such as La Roncière and Les Perrières on the south part which are very similar to La Richemone in the north, by virtue of the lighter soil with more stone than clay. If quality is to be measured by weight of flavour, then the two vineyards that compete for the first prize are Les Vaucrains and Les St Georges, with Les Pruliers close behind. Les Cailles and Les Porets are also front-runners.

Nuits is a most important centre for the Burgundian *négoce*, as in Beaune, albeit on a somewhat smaller scale. It too has its own Hospices, with vineyards of around ten hectares, and an annual auction of its wines in the spring.

I always feel that there ought to be more good wine from Nuits-St Georges than there is. It may be that the vineyards do not have as much potential as those of Gevrey; nonetheless, for a famous commune of large size, Nuits has a roll call of top growers that seems half as long as it should be. I suspect that the influence of the *négociants* has dimmed the town's perspectives and blunted the winemakers' potential.

Top Premiers Crus

Les Cailles	La Richemone
Aux Chaignots	La Roncière
Les Damodes	Les St Georges
Les Perrières	Les Vaucrains
Les Porets	Aux Vignes Rondes
Les Pruliers	

Good Nuits-St Georges producers

Robert Chevillon*	Domaine Machard de
Robert Dubois & Fils	Gramont
Domaine Faiveley	Alain Michelot*
Domaine Henri Gouges	Henri Remoriquet
	Domaine Daniel Rion*

CÔTE DE NUITS-VILLAGES

This appellation is not, as one might be forgiven for supposing, a general name open to all the villages of the Côte de Nuits to use for their basic wines. That would be too rational for Burgundy. In fact the name has been allocated to wines from the five villages of Corgoloin, Comblanchien, Prissey, Brochon and Fixin, only the last of which has the option of using its own name for its wines. (The wines of the southern half of Brochon have the right to the use of the Gevrey-Chambertin appellation.) It might have been logical to allow the use of the Côte de Nuits-Villages name for the wines of Couchey and Marsannay in the north, and indeed protracted efforts were made by their growers to apply for that right. But the idea met with bitter opposition from the other five villages, and yet again logic was defeated by self-interest. As it happens, the growers of Marsannay have now won their fight by gaining the right to use the individual commune name itself, though the Côte de Nuits-Villages appellation might have proved more useful to them in commercial terms.

At the southernmost end of the Côte de Nuits, the village of Comblanchien is more famous for its stone quarries than for its wine: Comblanchien marble has been used in the building of the Opéra in Paris, and more recently Orly airport. Corgoloin is an important centre for the production of Crème de Cassis. No doubt there are sites capable of yielding wines respectable enough to stand up to a modest Nuits-St Georges, but it is not surprising that it has been found easier to market the wines under the Côte de Nuits banner than under the actual commune name. (Indeed it is a pretty fair bet that in the last century most of Corgoloin's wine used to be sold as Pommard or Nuits, since the two major vineyard proprietors lived in those villages and their Corgoloin wines were vinified under the same roof, if not in the same vat, as their other wines.) Côtes de Nuits-Villages wines are recommended for early drinking, in the charm of their youth, since the vineyards concerned lack the ageing potential of Premiers Crus.

Good Côte de Nuits-Villages producers

Bernard Chevillon, Corgoloin
André Chopin & Fils, Comblanchien
Robert Dubois & Fils, Premeaux
Maurice Fornerol, Corgoloin
Jean Petitot, Corgoloin
Domaine de la Poulette, Corgoloin

THE CÔTE DE BEAUNE

The Côte d'Or may be compared to an opera in two acts. Technically, the curtain does not fall on act one, the Côte de Nuits, until we have passed through Comblanchien and Corgoloin; but it was Nuits-St Georges that provided the great final aria. When the curtain rises on act two, the drama is unchanged, but the set has altered. The slope has become broader, less steep in inclination, and it inclines more to the south. As for the soil, it too has undergone a slight change, becoming so much lighter in places that it is better suited to the white Chardonnay grape than the Pinot Noir.

LADOIX-SERRIGNY

If we continue the operatic analogy, and allow the first aria in this act to be sung by Aloxe-Corton, then Ladoix, or Ladoix-Serrigny to give it its proper commune title, provides the overture. The music gets more exciting the closer one gets to the Grand Cru *climats* of Corton-Renardes and Bressandes. Otherwise the general standard is decent but the wines have been easier to sell as Côte de Beaune-Villages than as Ladoix. There are signs that local confidence in its identity is growing, however, and it may be that the market will hear more of this name in the future as a good value substitute for the wines of Aloxe. At present the village's appellations are somewhat confused, the best *crus* qualifying for the Grand Cru Corton and Premier Cru Aloxe-Corton appellations, while those less well-sited qualify as Ladoix-Côte de Beaune, or as Côte de Beaune-Villages. No doubt Ladoix would dearly love to join Aloxe in adding Corton to its name instead of Serrigny. Its northernmost vineyards have more in common with the Côte de Nuits-Villages than with the appellations to the south, as might be expected from the geological similarities they share. Ladoix-Serrigny wines, in general, age well.

Good Ladoix-Serrigny producers	
Chevalier Père & Fils	Prince de Mérode
Edmond Cornu	Domaine André
Domaine Michel	Nudant & Fils
Mallard & Fils	

ALOXE-CORTON

This village is dominated by the prominent landmark of the hill of Corton, capped by its dark wood perched above an impressive array of vineyards beneath. On the lighter stony limestone soil just below the wood are the Chardonnay vines that produce Corton-Charlemagne, one of Burgundy's greatest white wines. Further round, facing east, we find redder earth with an iron content well suited to the Grand Cru Pinot Noir vineyards of Corton, the only Grand Cru vineyard for red wine on the whole of the Côte de Beaune, and also the largest Grand Cru in the whole of Burgundy. Lesser Aloxe wines are from deeper soils at lower levels, with an alluvial base containing some sand.

The wines of Aloxe are characterized by greater tannin levels than elsewhere in the Côte de Beaune and they are correspondingly capable of ageing very well, with Cortons of a good vintage lasting forty years and more. Indeed in their youth they are liable to seem hard. Opinions vary as to which *climat* gives the best wine. Some prefer the opulent perfumes and almost buttery flavours of Bressandes; others have a weakness for the rather special, more animal tastes of Renardes; while the very name Clos du Roi suggests some sort of historical basis for the superior reputation of that *climat*.

It is worth noting that the section of the vineyard designated 'Le Corton' is not to be thought of as superior to its neighbours, or accorded the same pre-eminent status as that held by Le Chambertin or Le Montrachet. I have had particularly satisfying bottles of Corton-Bressandes, but for sheer longevity Corton-Clos du Roi would probably take the honours. The most widely available wine is the famous Corton-Grancey from Louis Latour but good as that may be, there is undoubtedly more to the character of this worthy Grand Cru than is usually found in that particular example. Corton addicts will search out the wines that are less easy to lay one's hands on. Of the excellent Premiers Crus, for example, the proximity of Valozières and Maréchaudes to Bressandes is propitious and a good wine merchant would look out for a grower with vines in the highest part of these *climats*.

ALOXE-CORTON	
Top Grands Crus	**Top Premiers Crus**
Le Corton	Les Maréchaudes (part)
Corton-Bressandes	Les Valozières (part)
Corton-Clos du Roi	
Corton-Renardes	
Les Maréchaudes (part)	

Good Aloxe-Corton Producers

Domaine Adrien Belland
Domaine Chandon de Briailles
Domaine Louis Chapuis
Domaine Antonin Guyon
Domaine Daniel Senard*
Domaine Tollot-Beaut*

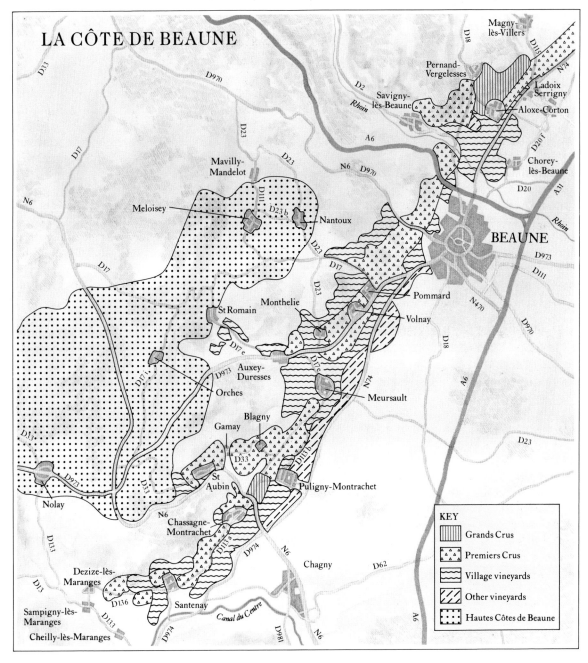

LA CÔTE DE BEAUNE

*The hill of Corton, crowned by its dark wood, is a dominant landmark. Its vineyards
are responsible for the only Grand Cru appellation for red wines in the Côte de Beaune.*

PERNAND-VERGELESSES

The relative obscurity of this commune is variously
attributed to its name, whose five sweet-sounding syl-
lables are thought to be too much for the non-profes-
sional to pronounce, and to its location, which is far
enough off the beaten track to deter the casual wine-
buyer and tourist. The village is behind the hill of
Corton, whose Grands Crus it shares with Aloxe-
Corton and Ladoix-Serrigny. But its share of Grand
Cru vineyard is more suited to the white Corton-
Charlemagne than to red Corton, for its exposure is
southwesterly and the soil contains less iron.

At their best, the red wines can age well, with a
somewhat harder style than the red wines of neighbouring Savigny. The most favourable Premier Cru
for red wine is the Ile des Vergelesses, by virtue of
the iron and clay in the soils there. (A similar case can
be argued for Les Fichots.) The village wines are
often sold as Côte de Beaune-Villages, for the usual
reason: it is commercially easier to sell wine from a
lesser-known commune by a well-known name. But
if you do happen upon a village Pernand-Vergelesses, you can expect as much charm and finesse as a
Savigny-lès-Beaune, and almost certainly more staying power. The village vineyards certainly have the
potential to produce good burgundy with the rare
advantage that the wine may actually be relatively
inexpensive.

Top Premiers Crus	
Ile des Vergelesses	Les Fichots

Good Pernand-Vergelesses producers	
Domaine Bonneau du Martray	Domaine Dubreuil-Fontaine
Domaine Chandon de Briailles	Domaine Laleure-Piot
Domaine Chanson	Domaine Louis Latour
Denis Père & Fils	Domaine Rapet Père & Fils

SAVIGNY-LÈS-BEAUNE

The villages of the Côte are more famous for the quality of their wines than the beauty of their situation. Indeed in the latter respect most are unremarkable. Savigny-lès-Beaune is an exception. It is both large enough and pretty enough to cater for the ordinary tourist as well as the wine connoisseur. The village has an attractive situation at the entrance to the Combe de Fontaine-Froide, a thoroughly charming valley in spite of its rather chilly-sounding name. A small trout stream, the Rhoin, meanders and gushes its way down from the hamlet of Bouilland to the north until it emerges into the plain. As it sweeps on beyond Savigny, it separates the appellation into two, leaving a number of *climats* on the Pernand side to the north and the rest on the Mont Battois above Beaune to the south. These two hillsides offer different soils and exposures. Although this fact is reflected in their respective wines, there is a common denominator to the wines of Savigny: they are as easy for the palate to appreciate as the village itself is for the eye to enjoy. Their precocious charms and wide availability make them less demanding on the concentration and the pocket than the wines of more illustrious communes. The best vineyards on the Pernand side, mostly south-facing (unusually for the Côte d'Or) are Aux Vergelesses, Les Lavières and Aux Guettes. The soil here is mixture of clay and oolitic limestone with iron. This produces a heavier, harder wine than do Les Marconnets, La Dominode and Les Peuillets on the opposite slopes, which face northeast and are composed of lighter, more gravelly soils with more sand. The ordinary village wines on the flatter land between the two slopes have less finesse, the soil being slightly less well-drained. In general, the wines of Savigny make up in perfume for what they lack in power. They are a sound choice for the restaurant trade.

Top Premiers Crus	
La Dominode	Les Marconnets
Aux Guettes	Aux Vergelesses

Good Savigny-lès-Beaune producers	
Simon Bize & Fils*	Pierre Guillemot
Jean-Marie Capron-Manieux	Domaine Antonin
Domaine Chandon de Briailles*	Guyon
Girard-Vollot & Fils	Pavelot-Glantenay

CHOREY-LÈS-BEAUNE

On the face of it, Chorey looks to be at some disadvantage, lying east of the Route Nationale, on flat land at a low altitude of around 230 metres, with soil that is alluvial debris from the valleys behind Savigny and Aloxe. It would appear to be a natural candidate for frost damage.

Not surprisingly, there are no Premiers Crus and most of the wine has been traditionally sold as Côte de Beaune-Villages. Yet it has been planted with vines since time immemorial. Perhaps its growers have always made a good living supplying Passetoutgrain at a reasonable price for the populace of nearby Beaune, rather as their brethren in Marsannay catered for Dijon. The *climats* of Beaumonts and Les Ratosses lie to the west of the Route Nationale, and are thus an extension geographically and stylistically to the wines of Savigny; while Les Champs-Longs, on flat, sandy and stony soils east of the road, has more in common with Aloxe. A third style can be found in Les Crais and Le Poirier-Malchaussée, sited on white marl on a bank of gravel: these produce quite tannic, somewhat 'medicinal' wines. The vineyards of Chorey may be less fortunately sited than the more famous names of the Côte de Beaune, but they are attracting increasing attention from the amateur and are more and more likely to be found under the commune name in future. They can often be very good value for money.

Good Chorey-lès-Beaune producers
Domaine Tollot-Beaut*
Domaine Jacques Germain*

BEAUNE

Beaune's importance as a wine town in France is surpassed only by that of Bordeaux. But its geographical location – on major autoroutes that link the rest of Northern France, Great Britain, the Low Countries and Germany with the south – coupled with the fact that is an exceptionally pretty small town, means that the wine trade there is in danger of being overshadowed by tourism and commerce. But it is wine that has made its name internationally recognized. It is the home of the majority of Burgundy *négociants*, and within its walls lie the extensive, bottle-lined cellars of the trading houses that have done so much to make the region world-famous: Bouchard Père &

The annual charity wine auction of the Hospices de Beaune takes place every November in the impressive surroundings of Beaune's Hôtel-Dieu.

Fils, Chanson, Drouhin, Louis Jadot, Louis Latour, Patriarche, etc.

Beaune organizes an annual boost to its publicity and to the funds of its hospital on the third Sunday of November, when it stages the Hospices de Beaune charity auction. This sale, of the wines made from the 57.6 hectares of the vineyards that form the Domaine des Hospices, acts as something of a barometer for the Burgundy market in general – although it is the pattern of prices, rather than the actual figures, that indicates the relative esteem of the vintage. It is, after all, a charity auction and one must therefore expect to pay high prices for that, and also for the publicity that invariably falls on the individual purchasers.

The vineyard holdings themselves are the result of bequests to the Hospices and it is the names of various benefactors which are now used to identify the different *cuvées*, e.g. Doctor Peste, Nicolas Rolin, Maurice Drouhin, General Muteau, and so on. (It should be emphasized that these are blends of wines from the same commune, but they are not single grower's wines in the true sense.) While the care and expertise of the actual vinification of the Hospices' wines need not normally be called into question, the subsequent *élevage* is a different matter, for it becomes the responsibility of the new owner – the purchaser at the auction. It is thus vital when buying one of these wines to check the name of the firm responsible for the bottling. The Hospices label by itself is no guarantee of quality.

One should not expect to find many bargains among these wines. Buying them would be less risky if they were 'estate-bottled', like all the greatest wines in Burgundy. But that seems unlikely to happen, as the present system works so successfully and conveniently from the point of view of those in charge.

Beaune's vineyards may be the property of the biggest names in the trade, but they do not make the greatest wines on the Côte d'Or by any stretch of the imagination. They are traditionally thought of as honest, straightforward wines of quality that will not disappoint. They are unlikely to generate heady excitement, but will usually bring pleasure and satisfaction. There are only about a dozen growers in this large commune outside the big *négociants'* domaines, so perhaps that factor has cut down the number of wines with real individuality of character.

The vineyards are argillo-calcareous, the better Premiers Crus occupying lighter soils at the top of the slopes, while the village wines are from deeper soil further down, with more clay and less stones. Those on the Savigny side of the appellation, like Grèves and Marconnets, tend to be firmer and develop less rapidly than those nearer Pommard, such as Boucherottes. The Clos des Mouches, almost a *monopole* of Joseph Drouhin, is planted with Chardonnay on the whiter soils at the top of its slope, while red wines are made from Pinot Noir grown on the browner soil of the lower half. There are thirty-nine Premiers Crus, so it is not easy to make a shortlist of the best.

Top Premiers Crus	
Les Boucherottes	Les Epenottes
Les Bressandes	Les Fèves
Les Cent Vignes	Les Grèves
Champs Pimont	Les Marconnets
Le Clos de la Mousse	Les Teurons
Le Clos des Mouches	Les Vignes Franches
Clos du Roi (part)	

Good Beaune producers
Domaine Arnoux Père & Fils
Domaine Besancenot-Mathouillet
Bouchard Père & Fils
Domaine Chanson Père & Fils
Domaine Joseph Drouhin*
Domaine Jacques Germain*
Domaine Louis Jadot*
Domaine Albert Morot

POMMARD

Pommard is much more to the marketing men's taste than, for example, Pernand-Vergelesses is. For the name rolls roundly off the tongue, especially in the USA, as does the wine – which usually lacks something in elegance and subtlety. It has more of the brash confidence of Gevrey-Chambertin than the refinement of its neighbour Volnay. The name is easy to pronounce and remember; more so than the wines, perhaps. I would avoid a *négociant*'s basic Pommard at all costs, and save up instead for a wine from one of the indisputedly fine Premiers Crus, such as Rugiens. For if basic Pommard can often be disappointingly commercial stuff, at the top of the scale there are Premiers Crus that are deserving of Grand Cru status, making them perhaps the best in the Côte de Beaune south of Corton. A reclassification might

elevate Les Rugiens Bas and parts of Les Grands Epenots, while in the right hands, excellent wine comes from Les Fremiets and Les Jarollières. The *monopole* of the Clos de la Commaraine is the jewel in the otherwise rather undistinguished crown of the large firm of Jaboulet-Vercherre. The secret with good Pommard is to allow it plenty of bottle age, for when young its strength can make it seem awkward; its charm and panache emerge only later, after cellaring. It should appeal to those who are fond of game and good Châteauneuf-du-Pape.

Top Premiers Crus	
Les Arvelets	Les Grands Epenots
Les Rugiens	Les Jarollières
Les Fremiets	Les Pézerolles

Good Pommard producers	
Domaine de Courcel	Domaine Mussy
Domaine Michel Gaunoux*	Domaine Parent*
Domaine Lejeune	Domaine Pothier-Rieusset
Domaine de Montille*	

VOLNAY

The village of Volnay enjoys an excellent view eastwards across the plains. On a few days every year it is even clear enough to see Mont Blanc in the distance. The vine has been cultivated here since Gallo-Roman times, while in the Middle Ages Volnay was the favourite summer residence of the Dukes of Burgundy, who no doubt appreciated the fine view, the clean air, the pure water and the excellent wine. The Marquis d'Angerville's Premier Cru Clos des Ducs is a testament to their affection.

Its red wines reach a higher general standard of quality than those of any other village on the Côte de Beaune, with a reputation in particular for elegance and finesse. These wines are rarely, if ever, coarse, and the general level of winemaking in the village is more serious than that found elsewhere; consequently there are fewer disappointments here than in most Burgundian appellations. They are wines of admirable balance.

This elegance in the wine is a reflection of the increasing lightness of the soil, for this village marks the point on the Côte de Beaune after which white wines outshine reds, as the next-door communes of Meursault and Puligny testify. Indeed, the most vivid overlap comes in the single Meursault *climat* of

Volnay is justifiably proud of its elegant wines. Their consistency and high standards are unmatched by any other village on the Côte d'Or.

Santenots, where the red wines are called Volnay and the white wines Meursault.

On the north side, Les Fremiets gives a wine similar to the adjacent Premiers Crus of Pommard, with a hard core masked by a fragrant exterior, and to a lesser extent the same can be said of the wines from the centre of the village, such as the Clos de la Bousse d'Or (the name is derived from the local dialect *bousse torre*, meaning *bonne terre* – good earth). The best of the Premiers Crus, though, are Clos des Chênes, Caillerets and Champans: all have a well-developed bouquet, complex perfume and great finesse on the palate, with a carefully vinified Caillerets from old vines the finest of all.

Top Premiers Crus	
Caillerets	Clos des Ducs
Champans	Les Fremiets
Clos de la Bousse d'Or	Santenots (in Meursault)
Clos des Chênes	Taille Pieds

Good Volnay producers	
Domaine Marquis d'Angerville	Domaine Michel Lafarge*
Pierre Boillot	Domaine des Comtes Lafon*
Domaine Y. Clerget	Domaine de Montille*
Domaine Bernard Glantenay	Domaine de la Pousse d'Or*

MONTHELIE

Pretty little Monthelie, the smallest village of the Côte de Beaune, is easily overlooked and hardly features on the wine lists of the world. It is no doubt used to having its wines sold as Volnay for red and Meursault for white, or as Côte de Beaune-Villages.

Viticulturally, it can be divided into two parts: Le Coteau de Volnay and La Vallée d'Auxey-Duresses. The former is composed of mixed limestone soil and red earth and is the location for the village's Premiers Crus, most notably Les Champs Fulliot, a neighbour of Volnay's Caillerets. The latter is formed of white limestone and, with vines exposed to both east and west, gives wines of a quite different style: heavier, but with finesse. If Monthelie has less class than Volnay, its wines are attractive nonetheless; while they are generally drunk young, the best can age well. The white wine production is negligible.

Top Premier Cru
Les Champs Fulliot

Good Monthelie producers	
Jacques Boigelot	Henri Potinet-Ampeau
Eric Boussey	Eric de Suremain

AUXEY-DURESSES

This village lies up the valley behind Meursault and produces both red and white wine, in the proportions of two-thirds to one-third respectively. The best of the red wine is grown on the Montagne du Bourdon which is the next hillside on from Monthelie, and the whites come from the opposite hillside to the south, the Coteaux du Mont Melian, adjacent to Meursault. While the whites do not repay keeping as long as good Meursault, the reds are quite hard when young, as the village name and that of one of its Premiers Crus, Les Duresses, would suggest; therefore they need to be kept some time if they are to soften and show at their best. The soil on Les Duresses is very thin and stony, especially higher up the slope, and is largely east-facing, by comparison with the vineyard of Le Val which faces squarely south. The limestone content of all the vineyards is considerable. In the past, the wines would have been sold as Pommard and Volnay. More recently, the Côte de Beaune-Villages appellation has been used, with improved legitimacy. If Les Duresses has a style similar to Volnay, then La Chapelle and Le Val are perhaps closer to Pommard, having more body and needing more time to mature. When the wines have enough depth of fruit to avoid the charge of meanness, they can represent fair value for money.

Top Premiers Crus	
Les Duresses	Le Val

Good Auxey-Duresses producers	
Jean-Pierre Diconne	Domaine du Duc de
Henri Latour	Magenta
Domaine Leroy	Bernard Roy
	Michel Prunier

SAINT ROMAIN

Round the corner and out of view at the end of its little valley, St Romain is further off the beaten track than any other Côte d'Or village and gives the impression of being about thirty years behind the times – although nowadays even the St Romain chickens have to scatter to make way for the odd Mercedes. It has a picturesque as well as a geographical affinity with the Hautes Côtes.

There is slightly more red wine produced here than white, although the latter has a better reputation. The soil is argillo-calcareous and stony, generally similar for both the red and white vineyards, though the exposure of the vineyards is variable. The site is well-protected from the wind and is relatively free of humidity and consequent rot. The whites make excellent apéritif wines, best when young and fresh, while the reds are fruity, vivacious wines with an aroma of cherries or strawberries. There are no Premiers Crus and none of the large *négociants* has a presence here. In fact, the most famous name in St Romain is probably that of François Frères, the cooper whose fine oak barrels are found in all the best cellars – from those of the Domaine de la Romanèe-Conti to Robert Mondavi's in California.

Good St Romain producers	
Alain Gras	Domaine René Thévenin-
Taupenot Père & Fils	Monthelie

The villages of St Aubin and St Romain lie up little valleys leading away from the main côte. This view from St Romain looks eastwards towards Meursault.

BLAGNY

It is easy to overlook Blagny, dwarfed as it is by the two giants of Côte de Beaune white wine production – Meursault and Puligny-Montrachet. The village itself, or rather hamlet, produces both red and white wines, but the real peculiarity of the appellation is that the name Blagny is the only one allowed for the red wines. While the white wines, from the *climats* of La Pièce sous le Bois, La Jeunelotte and Sous le Dos d'Ane are entitled to be called Meursault Premier Cru, the reds are Blagny Premier Cru. Correspondingly, the *climats* on the south side – Sous le Puits, La Garenne, Hameau de Blagny and Le Trézin – produce Puligny-Montrachet if white, but Blagny if red. (It is worth noting, however, that the appellation Meursault-Blagny for white wine was in use up to 1977.) In stylistic terms, Blagny's red wines can be recommended to those who are looking for individuality and distinct *goût de terroir* (an earthy flavour) in their wines. This makes direct comparison with other Côte d'Or wines difficult, but I do not mean to suggest that they are inferior in any way. On the contrary: their reputation is excellent and their price generally reasonable.

Top Premiers Crus	
La Pièce sous le Bois	Sous le Dos d'Ane

Good Blagny producers	
Robert Ampeau	Joseph Matrot
Domaine de Blagny	

CHASSAGNE-MONTRACHET

Nowadays this village is best known for its white wines, by virtue of the fact that it has linked its name with Le Montrachet. But it is worth recalling that it was the red wines that first created the reputation of the village. It was once said that only red wine producers here could afford soft white bread, and their white wine-producing neighbours had to make do with the hard brown or black variety; supporting evidence records that for many years one bottle of red Morgeot was worth two of Le Montrachet! Nowadays you could expect to get at least half-a-dozen bottles of the red for a single bottle of the world's most expensive dry white.

In quantity, the commune produces slightly more red wine than white, and much of it is undeniably fine, although none is officially found worthy of Grand Cru status. The better sites for the red wines are found on the slopes to the south of the village, where there is both limestone marl and red gravel. Le Morgeot and La Boudriotte provide the most powerful of the Premier Cru red wines, reminiscent more perhaps of the Côte de Nuits than the Côte de Beaune. They have a characteristic aroma of cherries, similar to that found in Nuits-St Georges, but lack the perfume and finesse of Vosne-Romanée.

There are some relatively large estates in the commune, notably those of Ramonet and Morey. The family names here frequently find themselves intertwined in a round-dance of permutations: Gagnard-Delagrange, Delagrange-Bachelet, Bachelet-Ramonet, Ramonet-Prudhon, and so on.

Top Premiers Crus	
La Boudriotte	Le Morgeot
Clos St Jean	

Good Chassagne-Montrachet producers	
Domaine Bachelet- Ramonet	Delagrange Domaine Morey
Domaine Carillon	Domaine Ramonet- Prudhon
Domaine Gagnard-	

SAINT AUBIN

Like St Romain to its north, St Aubin lies up a valley off the main Côte de Beaune; its vineyards have a southeast to southwest exposure. Included in this commune is the hamlet of Gamay, which has given its name to the red grape variety responsible for the wines of Beaujolais. Not surprisingly, it is banned from mention in this Côte d'Or appellation.

St Aubin produces two or three times as much red wine as white. The red is a good, attractive wine, similar to that of Chassagne next door, though somewhat prettier and less powerful. This village provides a happy hunting ground for the red burgundy enthusiast who cannot or does not wish to pay more for famous names. The producers are extremely conscientious and the wines rarely disappointing, something that can be said of few other communes on the Côte d'Or.

The vineyards falls into two parts, one near Gamay on the Roche du May which geographically marks the end of the Côte d'Or, and another on the Montagne du Ban, which marks the start of a separate *massif* stretching westwards. The terrain is, as usual on the Côte de Beaune, characterized largely by limestone, with a mix of brown clay and calcareous rubble. If the best white wines (e.g. those from La Chatenière), are marked by a pronounced aroma of hazelnuts, the reds most commonly remind me of strawberries. The vineyard of Les Sous-Roche Dumay, though, produces quite powerful and tannic wines from its relatively deep soil.

Top Premiers Crus	
La Chatenière	Les Sous-Roche Dumay
Les Frionnes	

Good St Aubin producers	
Domaine Clerget	Domaine Roux Père & Fils
Domaine Hubert Lamy	Gérard Thomas
Henri Prudhon	

SANTENAY

Santenay aspires to being a fashionable spa, and it actually boasts a casino. As the final major wine producing village of the Côte d'Or, though, it is more famous for its wine than its water.

Unlike Chassagne, its white wines are generally insignificant in both quantity and quality, an exception being made for the Clos des Gravières. As for the reds, they defy generalization to a greater extent than in any other village, for the terrain is a picture of geological confusion and variety. The vineyards adjacent to Chassagne – la Comme and les Gravières

The sprawling commune of Santenay is situated at the southern end of the Côte d'Or.

than the generic title. It is, in particular, a useful name for *négociants* who wish to blend wines of various communes to produce a large volume of wine in a uniform style.

The appellation is generally spurned by growers in prestigious and well-known villages such as Volnay and Pommard, but it can be a godsend for the growers of Chorey-lès-Beaune, Ladoix-Serrigny, St Romain, St Aubin and Sampigny-lès-Maranges. It can be used only for the red wines of the Côte de Beaune, in spite of the important quantity of white wine produced here.

Separate mention should be made of the three small villages of Dezize-, Cheilly- and Sampigny-lès-Maranges, all of which have added to their own name that of the best vineyard in which they each have a share, Les Maranges. It is officially a Premier Cru, and its plot is adjacent to Santenay's Clos Rousseau. Reliable producers include the Domaine Bernard Bachelet of Dezize and Domaine Paul Chevrot of Cheilly.

Reliable Négociants in the Côte d'Or	
Bouchard Père & Fils	Joseph Faiveley,
Chanson Père & Fils,	Nuits-St Georges
Beaune	Louis Jadot, Beaune*
Joseph Drouhin,	Louis Latour, Beaune
Beaune*	Maison Leroy

THE HAUTES CÔTES

Another world of Burgundian viticulture is concealed in the hills and valleys that lie to the west behind the Côte d'Or. Only twenty years ago, the vineyards of the *Arrière-Côte* were facing extinction. In the Hautes Côtes' heyday in the last century, just before the first appearance of the phylloxera vine pest, nearly 5,000 hectares were planted with vines. Only 500 hectares remained in 1967. The crisis of phylloxera itself had been followed by repeated outbreaks of oidium and mildew; then the death blow was the influx of cheap wine from the Midi and Algeria, enthusiastically preferred to local wines by some of the *négociants.* The region offered no career for a young winegrower and few remained.

The possibility of a revival depended on incentives to produce high-quality wine that could hold its own with the lesser wines of the Côte d'Or. There was no future in continuing with the hybrid varieties, or the Gamay, both of which had been increasingly planted in the recent past. What was needed was a new start.

– are composed of limestone marl and gravel, as the latter name suggests. These are the best vineyards of the village. South of Santenay itself, apart from La Maladière and Clos Rousseau, the wines tend to have less finesse, and some are very disappointing. I used to consider that life was too short to drink Santenay! Fortunately, I was able to revise my opinions after tasting some splendid wines from la Comme, and I now tend to think that there are real bargains to reward the careful purchaser here. The predominant flavour, as in St Aubin, is of strawberries.

Top Premiers Crus	
Beauregard	Les Gravières
Le Clos de Tavannes	Clos Rousseau
La Comme	

Good Santenay producers	
Adrien Belland	Michel Clair
Château de la Charrière	Domaine Lequin-Roussot
(Jean Girardin & Fils)	Mestre Père & Fils

CÔTE DE BEAUNE-VILLAGES

Unlike the Côte de Nuits-Villages appellation, this one serves mainly as an alternative marketing title for villages all over the Côte de Beaune which find their commune name less of a commercial proposition

By 1960 it was becoming increasingly apparent that there was not enough good wine in Burgundy to go round. The international market was growing and the Côte d'Or was all but fully exploited. It therefore became necessary to convince the authorities that the *Arrière-Côte* had the potential to make wine worthy of its own Burgundian appellation.

A NEW ERA

This battle was won on August 4th, 1961 when the INAO created the appellations of Hautes Côtes de Nuits and Hautes Côtes de Beaune. This legal groundwork gave the growers hope and provided the incentive needed to attract a new generation of *vignerons*. There was a future for viticulture here once more. In 1968, the cooperative Caves des Hautes Côtes opened in a prominent position on the Route Nationale, at its southern exit from Beaune. The cooperative provided vital help to producers who lacked the means for investing in modern equipment for vinification and *élevage*, and who were not able to commercialize their wines. The cooperative now makes around a quarter of the total production and acts as an important flagship for this part of Burgundy. Overall, the quantity of wine produced has rapidly increased. In the fifteen years from 1968 to 1983, the Hautes Côtes de Nuits saw its production grow from 170 hectolitres to 13,123 hectolitres, while that of the Hautes Côtes de Beaune showed a comparable increase from 660 hectolitres to 16,889 hectolitres. The Hautes Côtes were back in business.

Controversial innovations in the field of viticultural methods have taken place, in particular the widespread introduction of a system of training the vines higher and increasing the space between the rows. The growers needed to make economies in the vineyard without risking a decline in quality. The new system of spacing and training would not have been effective or beneficial on the Côte d'Or, but in the Hautes Côtes, with their higher altitude, the experiments have proved a success: they facilitate mechanization, and eliminate much of the risk of frost damage. It should be recalled that the Hautes Côtes lie, as the name suggests, above as well as behind the main Côte, with an average altitude between 350 and 500 metres.

The soil structure of the sub-region is variable, but is characterized by a mix of limestone and clay similar to that found on the main Côte. A favourable orientation and good protection from the cold winds are of particular importance at these higher altitudes. If the wines are sometimes criticized for being light and thin, it is to some extent a reflection of this location. It may also be due to the relative youth of the vines concerned, for twenty-five-year-old vines here are the exception, not the rule. In this respect, the wines of the Hautes Côtes de Nuits can be lighter than those of the Hautes Côtes de Beaune, for the vineyards here are more recent still. Production in the Hautes Côtes de Beaune is considerably larger than in the Hautes Côtes de Nuits and much of it is from comparatively long-established vineyards. This gap will close with time, but it will take at least another decade. Similarly, it will need time for any individual communes from among the twenty-eight concerned to develop a particular reputation. At present their communal identity is more of a help than a hindrance to their marketing.

There is a good deal of public relations work still to be done before the general public and the world's wine importers are familiar with the wines of the Hautes Côtes, and the more dynamic *vignerons* are well aware of this. Accordingly, they have taken steps to attract more visitors, and with this in mind, the *Maison des Hautes Côtes* has been established at Marey-lès-Fussey. This building contains a restaurant in which to taste the wines and the food of the region. The growers hope that the combination of pretty countryside and attractive wines will prove a successful formula for future prosperity. It will be interesting to watch the growth in the reputation of the following villages and producers, in addition to that of the Caves des Hautes Côtes, based in Beaune.

Good Hautes Côtes de Nuits producers

Claude Cornu, Magny-lès-Villers
Domaine Fribourg, Villers-La-Faye
Geisweiler & Fils, Nuits-St Georges
Bernard Hudelot, Villars-Fontaine
Jayer-Gilles, Magny-lès-Villers
Henri Naudin-Ferrand, Magny-lès-Villers
Simon Fils, Marey-lès-Fussey
Domaine Thévenot-le-Brun, Marey-lès-Fussey
Alain Verdet, Arcenant

Good Hautes Côtes de Beaune producers

Jean-Claude Bouley, Nolay
Denis Carre, Meloisey
François Charles, Nantoux
Château de Mercey, Cheilly-lès-Maranges
Lucien Jacob, Echevronne
Jean Joliot, Nantoux
Domaine des Vignes des Demoiselles, Nolay

THE CÔTE CHALONNAISE AND THE MÂCONNAIS

The present increase in demand for Côte d'Or wines can only come as good news for producers in the less prestigious parts of Burgundy, for not everyone can afford the best, particularly when there is so little of it. If the future looks bright in backwaters such as the Hautes Côtes then it must look brighter still in areas as well established as the Côte Chalonnaise or the Mâconnais.

We have, so far, progressed southwards down the Côte d'Or to its conclusion at Santenay. The next stage in the journey covers the ground stretching from Chagny, the first important town south of Beaune, as far as Mâcon itself. This is a much larger area than the Côte d'Or, stretching across about 50 miles of mixed agricultural land on much of which there is not a vine to be seen.

These two districts of the Côte Chalonnaise and the Mâconnais lie to the west of the large towns from which they take their names, though the towns themselves boast no vineyards of their own and lie outside the delimited appellation areas. Whereas Mâcon lends its name to both red and white wines in its appellation (Mâcon Blanc, Rouge, -Villages, etc.), there is no such thing as Chalon Blanc or Rouge. The forty-three little villages of the Mâconnais, often no more than hamlets, tend to join their names to the mother-appellation (e.g. Mâcon-Viré, Mâcon-Clessé, etc.) but the four main villages of the Chalonnais have the size and confidence to market their wines under their individual commune names alone: Rully, Mercurey, Givry, Montagny. (Bouzeron is allowed the use of its own name only in conjunction with its Aligoté wines.)

THE CÔTE CHALONNAISE

Geographically and geologically, the Côte Chalonnaise is a fragmented extension of the Côte d'Or. There is no continuous single sweep of vineyard as in the north, but the soils are much the same, with plenty of limestone mixed into the clay. Two-thirds of the vineyard area is planted with Pinot Noir, the balance being taken up by Chardonnay, Aligoté and Gamay vines. Although the region lies to the south of the Côte d'Or, the climate can often be cooler, due to local factors.

BOUZERON

A village of minor significance, particularly for red wine; such fame as it enjoys is due to the quality of its Aligoté. There are two particularly good producers who have helped to put Bouzeron on the map: A & P de Villaine and Chanzy Frères. Aubert de Villaine is best known as a co-proprietor of the Domaine de la Romanée-Conti, but he is justifiably proud of his Aligoté from Bouzeron, and his Bourgogne Rouge is also commendable: correct and well made with some charm, though it would be wrong to expect greatness from it. Like most Chalonnais wines, I suspect, it has the virtue of offering excellent value for money rather than spectacular quality.

Good Bouzeron producers	
Chanzy Frères	A & P de Villaine*

RULLY

Rapid expansion is under way in Rully. At present, slightly more red wine is produced than white, although the white enjoys a better reputation. There are a lot of young Pinot Noir vines around in Rully at present, so perhaps the quality of the reds will catch up as the vines mature. Until then, the likelihood is that one will find them light, lacking in finesse and depth of fruit, and with an earthy, somewhat animal flavour, though there are notable exceptions to this rule from some of the growers found listed in the box below.

As an alternative to burgundy from the Côte de Beaune, Rully's red wine it is not quite as successful as the white, and should not generally be allowed too much in the way of bottle age. Rully has also a reputation for producing both red sparkling and white sparkling wines.

Good Rully producers
Jean-Claude Brelière
Domaine de la Folie (Xavier Noël-Bouton)*
H & P Jacqueson
Guy Mugnier
Domaine du Prieuré
Domaine de la Renarde (Jean-François Delorme)

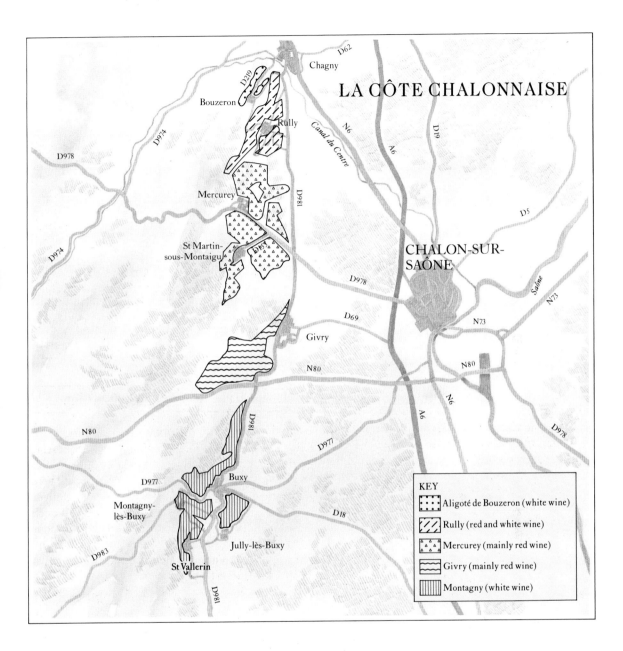

LA CÔTE CHALONNAISE

KEY

Aligoté de Bouzeron (white wine)

Rully (red and white wine)

Mercurey (mainly red wine)

Givry (mainly red wine)

Montagny (white wine)

MERCUREY

The Côte Chalonnaise has sometimes been referred to as the Région de Mercurey, an indication of this village's superiority in terms of both the quantity and the quality of its wines, about ninety-five per cent of which are red. Some have the depth and structure to permit serious comparison with more famous names in the Côte d'Or – there is a hint of cherries in certain wines that reminds me of Chassagne-Montrachet and Nuits-St Georges, for example. Others have compared them to a light Pomerol (from Bordeaux), so the reputation of the village is well-established and it

has not had to struggle for recognition in the same way as Rully, which for a long time passed off its red wines under the same label as its more prestigious neighbour, before it was forced by law to use its own identity. In the same way Mercurey itself has been almost a candidate for adoption by the Côte d'Or: up to seventy per cent of its production, which has more than tripled since 1945, has traditionally been sold through the *négociants* of Beaune and Nuits-St Georges. Mercurey is also sold in 228-litre casks, as in the Côte d'Or, whereas the traditional cask size of the Chalonnais and Mâconnais is 215 litres; and

*Château de Rully in the Côte Chalonnaise
dominates a slope of red soil:
the characteristic colour of Pinot Noir vineyard
earth throughout the entire Burgundy region.*

Mercurey insists on a lower maximum yield than the other communes of the Chalonnais, again inviting comparison with the Côte d'Or. More than fifty per cent of the vineyard area is in the hands of just half-a-dozen producers, Bouchard Aîné, Faiveley, Protheau and Rodet being the best known, but in addition to them there are at least 60 small producers, some of them producing excellent wine.

The local *confrérie* organizes an annual tasting to approve a selection of the best wines of the commune. The selected bottles are then entitled to bear the words *Chante Flûté* on their labels.

Premiers Crus

Clos des Fourneaux	Clos Marcilly
Clos des Montaigus	Clos Voyen
Clos du Roi	

Note, though, that these *crus* do not necessarily produce the best wines. The producer is of equal importance, and certain estates have particularly good vineyards that are not officially classified as Premiers Crus, such as Michel Juillot's Clos des Barraults.

Good Mercurey producers

Luc Brintet & Frédéric Charles
Domaine Faiveley
Jeannin-Naltet Père & Fils
Michel Juillot*
Yves & Paul de Launay
Louis Menand Père & Fils
Domaine de la Monette (Paul-Jean Granger)
Domaine Saier
Domaine de Suremain*

GIVRY

Givry lies to the south of Mercurey, the other side of a vine-free zone of about ten kilometres. Historically, its reputation has been established for centuries: it enjoyed its heyday in the Middle Ages, and continued to sell its wine for a higher price than Mercurey through to the end to the nineteenth century. Now, though, it gives the impression of being in something of a decline, and even its claim to being the favourite wine of Henri IV will not rescue it from the urban growth of Chalon, nor will the fact that its wines are at best agreeable rather than remarkable. (Henri IV was not known as a great arbiter of taste, and it is a safe bet that his patronage extended towards anything with alcohol in it.) As has already been noted, incentives are commercially vital if good wine

is to be made, and in the case of the growers of Givry, it looks as if the incentives provided by property developers may well prevail over those offered by winemaking. There are, however, a small band of dedicated producers who will, no doubt, succeed in protecting the red (and tiny quantities of white) wines of Givry from extinction. The *négociant* Louis Latour has an important leasehold here, and about a quarter of the entire appellation is exploited by the Domaine du Baron Thénard. There are also a number of good small producers to help keep Givry's name on the map (see below).

Good Givry producers

Domaine Jean Chofflet
Propriété Desvignes
Domaine du Gardin (Clos Salomon)
Domaine Joblot
Lumpp Frères
Gérard Mouton
Bernard Tatraux
Domaine Thénard

MONTAGNY

Montagny is the most southerly appellation of the Côte Chalonnaise and the name is reserved exclusively for white wines. Three other villages fall within the appellation: Buxy, Jully-lès-Buxy and St Vallerin. A small amount of Bourgogne Rouge and Passetoutgrain is produced: while this does not have the individuality and class of the white Montagny, it is perfectly respectable when properly made. Apart from the efforts of good individual growers (see below), it is worth looking out for Bourgogne Rouge from the excellent small *négociant-éleveurs* B and J-M Delaunay, for it will have been carefully selected and expertly made.

Good Montagny producers

Cave des Vignerons de Buxy
Bernard Michel
Veuve Steinmaier & Fils
Jean Vachet

THE MÂCONNAIS

A short drive further south from the Chalonnais brings one into the vineyards of the Mâconnais, a region of much larger production of both red and white wine than its northern neighbour. In Louis

XIV's time it was best known for red wines, but the reverse is true nowadays. Two distinct soil types exist: where calcareous soils predominate the Chardonnay thrives, while more sand and clay in the soil favours red wine production from Gamay and, to a lesser extent, Pinot Noir. About two-thirds of the total volume is white wine, reflecting the current fashion for white as much, perhaps, as actual quality, and while Mâcon can bathe to some extend in the reflected glory of Pouilly Fuissé, there is no comparably famous *cru* to help boost the cause of the red wines. From the quality angle, red Mâcon is overshadowed by the Beaujolais, which not only makes much more wine, but is generally better at emphasizing the fruity charms of the Gamay grape. No doubt its well-drained granite-based soils are much more suitable in this respect than the chalky clay of the Mâconnais. Vinification techniques for the red wine also resemble those of Beaujolais (see page 69) rather than the Côte d'Or.

Over half the production of the area is in the hands of the region's competent cooperatives. There are seventeen or so of them situated in villages such as Lugny, Viré, Igé, and Clessé. Their wine is frequently better than that of the average grower. On the other hand, there are a small number of growers with skill and a privileged site who make the best wines of their region. While I find Mâcon Rouge made from the Gamay generally disappointing if compared with a good Beaujolais, the region's Pinot Noir is capable of varietal character and depth of flavour in a good vintage. Perhaps growers in the Mâconnais should concentrate on Chardonnay and Pinot Noir and acknowledge that Beaujolais has them beaten when it comes to Gamay. Too often Mâcon Rouge tastes like an indifferent *vin ordinaire* and its right to an *Appellation Contrôlée* seems based more on historic reasons than on any inherent quality in the wine itself.

Good Mâconnais producers
Domaine de Chervin, Burgy Domaine Guffens-Heynen, Vergisson Pierre & Véronique Janny, Peronne Henri Lafarge, Bray

A vineyard in the Mâconnais, best known for white wine. Some good Bourgogne Rouge is made from Pinot Noir there, as well as rather less worthwhile Mâcon Rouge made from Gamay.

BEAUJOLAIS

After the complexities and paradoxes of the Côte d'Or, it is something of a relief to proceed to Beaujolais, forsaking the glamour, class and de luxe price tags of Vosne and Volnay, and substituting in their place wines of easy appeal, made from an unpretentious grape in the happy surroundings of its natural habitat. The wines are frank and thirst-quenching, as undemanding on the brain as they are easy on the pocket, and few, if any, need to be laid down for long. The importance of knowing the individual grower is also of less significance than in the Côte d'Or, for the vast bulk of the wine is sold by merchants and cooperatives, not by individual growers. It is not necessary, therefore, for the customer to try and memorize nearly so many names. The wine itself presents relatively few problems to the grower or the winemaker, so unpalatable surprises are uncommon; and there is plenty of it, so the potential purchaser should not encounter many difficulties in finding what he or she wants. The main problem for the prospective buyer may be in navigation, for the lanes here are masterpieces of the art of directional deception. The consolation is that there can be few prettier places than Beaujolais in which to get lost.

Proceed with caution though. There is a strong possibility that the local driver coming the other way, on either side of the road, has something rather above the already impressive national average for wine consumption in his bloodstream. My own experience as a passenger of a one-armed, 'Beaujolais-for-breakfast' tractor driver during the grape harvest always makes me take more than ordinary care when using the roads of the region. It is an area of more gulping than spitting. The alcohol got the better of that same tractor driver one night, when he announced his intention – after a minor misunderstanding – of killing an amiable German student who was grape-picking with the rest of us. Frequent appeals by the tractor driver down in the courtyard for the *patron* met with silence from that quarter and abuse from ours, since we wanted our sleep after the backbreaking labours of the day. After breaking a pane of glass behind my head, he vented his frustration at not being able to find and dispose of his intended victim by taking off all his clothes and walking five miles to Villefranche stark naked through a torrential downpour (1975 was a poor vintage in Beaujolais). He spent the rest of the night in police custody and returned to the harvest the next day, rather late and with a sheepish look. In some vineyards such incidents might have had serious repercussions but in Beaujolais the tendency is to laugh them off. It should also be stressed that the wine of this region is normally responsible for inspiring good-natured rather than bloodthirsty reactions to one's fellow human beings.

SOIL AND CLIMATE

The best parts of the Beaujolais are characterized by schistous and decomposed granite soils, light and well-drained. In the Bas-Beaujolais below Villefranche there is more clay and more limestone, and the soil is in general less well-drained. The altitude of the best vineyards lies between 200 and 350 metres and the optimum vineyard exposure in the region is south-southeast.

The climate of the Beaujolais is variously affected by Atlantic, Mediterranean and Continental influences. Depending on which influence is dominant at any time, the conditions can vary quite dramatically, with winters being cold or warm, spring wet or dry, and summers scorching with heat or damp with storms and frequent hail. The autumn, too, is inconsistent in its variation from dry and warm to cold and wet. The annual temperature variation ranges from an astonishing minus twenty degrees Celsius to forty degrees Celsius. Having said that, ripening grapes here is not generally a problem as uniformly poor summers are uncommon, unlike further north, on the Côte d'Or.

VITICULTURE

In contrast to the other regions of Burgundy, where Pinot Noir pruning is by the Guyot or Cordon-de-Royat systems, the method of pruning in the Haut-Beaujolais is the *gobelet* system, whereby each plant stands free and unsupported, forming its own little bush. For the Beaujolais *crus* and Beaujolais-Villages appellation the *gobelet* is stipulated by law, but the Guyot Simple system (training the vine along wires) can be, and indeed normally is, used for the basic Beaujolais.

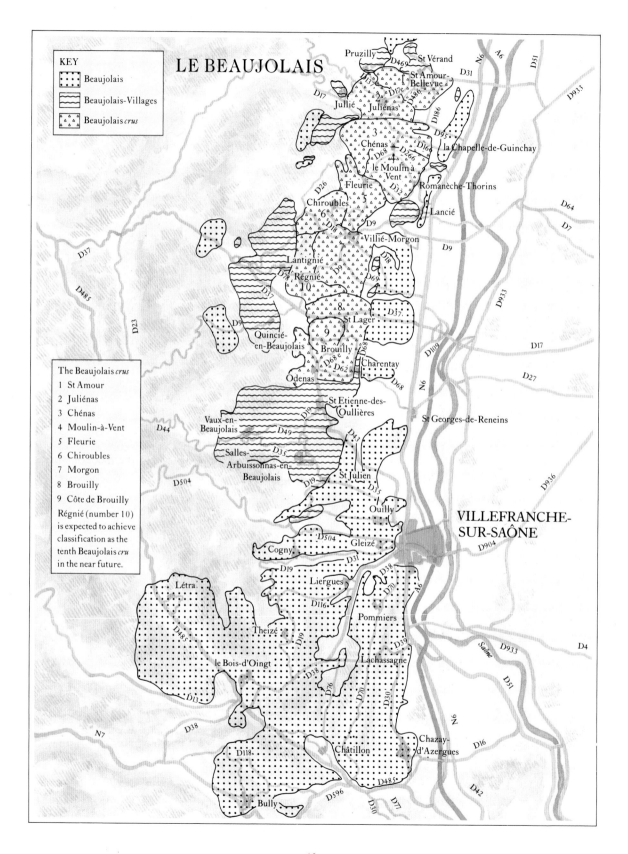

LE BEAUJOLAIS

KEY

Beaujolais

Beaujolais-Villages

Beaujolais *crus*

The Beaujolais *crus*
1 St Amour
2 Juliénas
3 Chénas
4 Moulin-à-Vent
5 Fleurie
6 Chiroubles
7 Morgon
8 Brouilly
9 Côte de Brouilly

Régnié (number 10) is expected to achieve classification as the tenth Beaujolais *cru* in the near future.

Pruzilly
St Vérand
St Amour-Bellevue
Jullié
Juliénas
la Chapelle-de-Guinchay
Chénas
le Moulin à Vent
Fleurie
Romanèche-Thorins
Chiroubles
Lancié
Villié-Morgon
Lantignié
Régnié
St Lager
Quincié-en-Beaujolais
Brouilly
Charentay
Odenas
St Etienne-des-Oullières
Vaux-en-Beaujolais
St Georges-de-Reneins
Salles-Arbuissonnas-en-Beaujolais
St Julien
Ouilly
VILLEFRANCHE-SUR-SAÔNE
Cogny
Gleizé
Létra
Liergues
Theizé
Pommiers
le Bois-d'Oingt
Lachassagne
Châtillon
Chazay-d'Azergues
Bully

VINIFICATION

The difference between Beaujolais and the rest of Burgundy in vinification terms lies in the tradition of vinifying the grapes uncrushed. The unbroken grapes are put into vats, ideally of no more than sixty hectolitres. The weight of the grapes breaks the skins of those at the base of the pile and releases their juice. The yeasts that naturally occur on grape skins then initiate fermentation. The carbonic gas given off during this process encourages the subsequent fermentation of the juice within the grapes above, while at the same time acting as an anti-oxidant. At an ideal temperature of between twenty-five and twenty-eight degrees Celsius, the fermentation lasts for about a week. After the free-run juice (*vin de goutte*) is taken from the vat, the grapes are pressed and the resulting juice (*vin de presse*), which may be two-thirds of the total, is blended in with the free-run. This is in contrast to most normal red wine vinification, where the press wine is a small percentage of the total. The process as a whole is perfectly natural, tailor-made for emphasizing the attractive characteristics of the Gamay grape. This same basic system is used for most, if not all, wines from Beaujolais, though it is modified with a longer vatting time, to provide greater body and power in the better *cru* wines.

Bottling for the Nouveau wines takes place in mid-November, while for the other wines it can happen any time between January and the middle of the summer. Most of the *crus* are bottled by the end of May.

THE GROWERS

Métayage or tenant farming is a marked feature of land tenure in Beaujolais. The harvest and certain expenses are shared on a fifty-fifty basis by the owner and the tenant-grower. The owner provides the land, the vines, and the materials while the tenant looks after the vineyard, makes the wine and gets half of the returns. Most Beaujolais properties are small, between five and ten hectares. There are eighteen co-operatives which account for around thirty per cent of the total production. About half the total production now is exported.

HAUT-BEAUJOLAIS AND BAS-BEAUJOLAIS

The Beaujolais district can be divided into two: the Haut-Beaujolais – extending from Mâcon to Villefranche-sur-Saône; and the Bas-Beaujolais – following on from there to the outskirts of Lyon, whose large population has always assured producers of a ready and accessible market.

The striking profile of the great limestone rock of Solutré marks the end of the Mâconnais and the start of the Beaujolais. It towers like a great wave over the vineyards of Mâcon's most celebrated appellation, Pouilly-Fuissé, which (with St Véran) is adjacent to the most northerly of the Beaujolais *crus*, St Amour. As the limestone gives way to granite, so the Chardonnay makes way for Gamay.

All the best Beaujolais wines, by which we mean those from the *crus* and the Beaujolais-Villages, come from the Haut-Beaujolais. Here you should be assured of a decent level of quality. In the Bas-Beaujolais, which extends almost as far south as Lyon, a huge increase in planting has recently taken place, not always on soils ideal for good wine, and consequently the quality is considerably less reliable. There is plenty of wine that seems to have more in common with *vin ordinaire* than with Beaujolais. It is the source of most Beaujolais Nouveau which, no doubt, accounts for the wide variation in the quality of that wine. Buying such wines is a waste of money, except in the case of Beaujolais Nouveau from a good grower or merchant in a good vintage. The Haut-Beaujolais soil of decomposed granite, on the other hand, should give wines with body, class and ageing potential.

BEAUJOLAIS NOUVEAU

Beaujolais has achieved one of the modern world's most remarkable marketing successes, and it repeats the achievement every year. In mid-November it sells, at a comfortable profit, around half the wine made in the vintage a few weeks before. The Beaujolais is experiencing a period of unprecedented prosperity as a result. The cash-flow advantages of this operation make the growers of other wine regions green with envy, and winemakers from Muscadet, the Midi, Italy, Australia and South Africa have all tried to create a similar market, but with limited success. It is Beaujolais that has managed to steal this particular show by making the most of its natural potential to do so. The secret lies in revealing the precocious charms of the Gamay grape through carbonic maceration, which highlights fruit and minimizes extraction of tannin.

Although most of the wine that goes to make Nouveau comes from the Bas-Beaujolais, some of the better wines are made from grapes that qualify for the Beaujolais-Villages appellation. It makes good sense to consume the lightest wines of the area fastest, so if you are looking for basic Beaujolais then you can probably do no better than select a good Nouveau.

The most successful vats are generally used for the Nouveau nowadays, which means that the poorest quality ones are liable to be sold as ordinary Beaujolais, later on, when the Nouveau's short season has finished. These are best avoided.

There is, generally, no reason to worry about good Nouveau needing to be drunk before Christmas. It will almost certainly keep and improve well beyond Easter and for up to a year from the vintage. I have drunk many bottles that were five or six years old and found them none the worse for the experience. So buyers of basic Beaujolais should taste and buy their whole year's requirements in late November.

The main disadvantage of what one might call the Nouveau vogue is not the gimmickry involved so much as the fact that it may restrict the amount of wine left for making into something very much better. It is a pity to see producers tempted by quick profits not making the best that could be achieved from their vineyards. Furthermore, if less good wine is being made, the price of the good wine which does reach the marketplace is bound to rise faster than it would normally do. In my opinion, the Nouveau craze has gone far enough and should not be allowed to exceed its natural limits of production, both geographic and commercial (production of Nouveau has quadrupled between 1970 and 1982).

THE APPELLATIONS

In total contrast to the situation on the Côte d'Or, appellations in Beaujolais have the great advantage of being few in number and simple to understand. There are no Premier Cru vineyards, just Beaujolais, Beaujolais Supérieur, Beaujolais-Villages and the individual *crus*. Furthermore, the distinction between Beaujolais and Beaujolais Supérieur is now practically meaningless and the latter is rarely used. In theory, it indicates higher natural alcohol: ten per cent for Beaujolais and ten-and-a-half per cent for Beaujolais Supérieur. The finished wines, though, tend to be bottled with twelve to thirteen-and-a-half degrees of alcohol in any case.

THE BEAUJOLAIS *crus*

From north to south, the ten names to remember are St Amour, Juliénas, Chénas, Moulin-à-Vent, Fleurie, Chiroubles, Morgon, Régnié (which is due to join the club in 1988), Brouilly and Côte de Brouilly. There are characteristics peculiar to each of these villages which distinguish their wines from one another, but it is the similarities that are increasingly in evidence. There is a growing tendency for individual hallmarks to be erased by blending. The popularity of the wine may in this respect be its downfall, for even in the *crus* producers are becoming complacent and rather less quality-conscious than they might be if they had more of a struggle to sell their wines.

Fortunately the individuality of the different *crus* is maintained by a handful of growers who bottle their own wines, and also by a few *négociant-éleveurs* who are careful to vinify the wines of each grower separately and thus avoid blurring the characteristics of the wines.

The larger *négociants* of the Côte d'Or frequently include a full range of Beaujolais in their portfolios, for it gives them the chance of offering useful cash-flow wines at lower prices. These wines are usually acceptable, but they are often marked by the *négociant*'s own house style rather more than by the character of the *cru*. Remember too that the *crus* of Beaujolais can have their wine declassified as Bourgogne Rouge. This is useful to the Côte d'Or *négociants*, but is downright misleading for the consumer as the appellation excludes Gamay in one area – the Côte d'Or and Côte Chalonnaise – but allows it in another.

The maximum permitted yield for the *crus* is forty-eight hectolitres per hectare, subject to modification according to the nature of the vintage.

SAINT AMOUR

St Amour was the ninth of the *crus* to gain recognition, its appellation dating from 1946. It thoroughly deserves its status. High standards are observed by all the growers here, and perhaps this is why a cooperative has never been founded in the village. It may also be why the name is not as well-known as it might be, for powerful cooperatives help promote names in a way that a large number of small growers cannot. It should, though, benefit from a sharp boom in sales around St Valentine's day, and no doubt its name attracts the romantically-inclined buyer at other times of the year. As for the wine, it is as pretty as the name suggests, with a delicacy shared by Fleurie and Chiroubles. The Coupe Dailly is awarded annually to the wine adjudged the best St Amour of the year. It is named after Louis Dailly, whose efforts were largely responsible for the elevation of St Amour to *cru* status. About 150,000 cases are produced from some 275 hectares (650 acres), making it one of the smaller *crus*. It is also the only *cru* that lies in the *département* of Saône-et-Loire as opposed to that of the Rhône. Being the nearest *cru* to Pouilly-Fuissé, it is not surprising to find a little limestone in the vineyards here. The white wines of the commune are entitled to the St Véran appellation. St Amour from a good vintage will be at its best after two or three years in bottle.

Good St Amour producers
Domaine des Billards (Ets Loron & Fils)
Domaine des Duc
Domaine Janin
Elie Mongénie
Domaine du Paradis (bottled by Maurice Delorme the proprietor, but also by Georges Duboeuf)
Domaine Patissier
Domaine Francis Saillant

JULIÉNAS

The 560 hectares of Gamay situated within this *cru* produce over 200,000 cases of reliable and satisfying wine with plenty of backbone and flesh, often making them the best balanced of all Beaujolais wines. The vineyards may well have been amongst the earliest planted in the region and the commune undoubtedly has a long history; it is alleged that it owes the ancient version of its name – Julienacas – to Julius Caesar. In addition to vivid fruit flavours in the wines, reminiscent of raspberries and cherries, there are sometimes extra spicy flavours that add another dimension to this most appealing wine. It is all too easy to drink when young, but maturity comes at five years and good vintages could happily last a lot longer. Juliénas has an annual custom that is entirely typical of the spirit of Beaujolais: each November there is a celebration of the new vintage at which a prize of one-hundred-and-four bottles of Juliénas are awarded to the person considered to have done most to promote the interests of the wine over the preceding year. This number ensures the winner two bottles of wine for each Sunday of the year, one for himself and one for his wife, though I'd be surprised if this ration lasted for half the time in a place like Beaujolais! In these times of ever-increasing yields perhaps the relevant committee should consider raising the quantity to a bottle a day. It is a commune whose wines rarely

The village of Juliénas produces wine that is frequently a match for the very best in Beaujolais. The wines of its finest growers, in particular, are always worth sampling.

disappoint and the names of the Juliénas producers given in the box below should prove well worth remembering.

Good Juliénas producers

Ernest Aujas
François Condemine (Château de Juliénas)
Domaine Gonon
Claude & Michelle Joubert
Domaine René Monnet
André Pelletier (Eventail)
Jacques Perrachon (Domaine de la Bottière)
Raymond & Michel Tête

CHÉNAS

With only 250 hectares under vines and an annual production of around 140,000 cases, Chénas is the smallest of the *crus*. The major reason for this is that a number of its vineyards are also eligible for the better-known, neighbouring appellation of Moulin-à-Vent. Many growers who have vineyards entitled to the use of both appellations opt for the Moulin-à-Vent label for their best *cuvées* and Chénas for the less good. This certainly explains why the reputation of Chénas is not as high as it might be. There are some bargains to be found here, though, because its lesser reputation means a more modest price. The best strategy is to find a producer who is proud enough of the appellation to allow its use for his best wine.

The producers of Moulin-à-Vent have in the past tried to convince the proprietors of Chénas of the wisdom of a takeover, to increase the output of Moulin-à-Vent. Fortunately the Chénas growers are sufficiently stubborn to resist such ideas. Chénas would do well to capitalize on its small size and limited availability. By making the best wine possible it could, in time, demand as high a price as its neighbour does. Small size is not necessarily a barrier to fame – often quite the contrary. The general style of the wines of the village is robust, and some wines need six years or more to reach maturity, while others are at their best much sooner. Because of its peculiar circumstances, it is a hard commune about which to generalize.

Good Chénas producers

Louis Champagnon	Pierre Perrachon (Château
Château de Chénas	Bonnet)
Gérard Lapierre	Daniel Robin
Hubert Lapierre	Jean-Louis Santé

MOULIN-À-VENT

This commune has the highest reputation of all the *crus*, by virtue of its power and longevity. It occupies 650 hectares within the communes of Chénas and Romanèche-Thorins and produces around 375,000 cases annually. There is no actual village of this name, just a sail-less windmill lying at an altitude of 240 metres. Its granite-based soil is rich in minerals such as manganese, giving great depth of colour and flavour. Of all the *crus*, this is the one that is said to most resemble a Pinot Noir wine from northern Burgundy, if allowed to acquire sufficient bottle age. I once enjoyed a magnum of 1980 Moulin-à-Vent, though, that resembled not so much a Pinot Noir from the Côte d'Or as a Merlot from St Emilion in Bordeaux.

When young, Moulin-à-Vent can be relatively harsh, closed-in and uncharming by Beaujolais standards, hence it is a poor candidate for selling as a Nouveau. It has the depth and structure to support ageing even in new oak barrels. Nothing is more disappointing in a comparative tasting of Beaujolais than to find a Moulin-à-Vent that is as pale and pretty as young Beaujolais-Villages. Unfortunately such experiences are not uncommon nowadays, as easy profits encourage producers to cut corners and ignore the true potential of their raw material. It must, sadly, come as no surprise to find mediocre wines masquerading under the most famous name in the district. (It is worth noting in this context that the Moulin-à-Vent from Georges Duboeuf, while good as always, is relatively light and not particularly typical.) The *climats* of La Rochelle and La Tour du Bief, both from the Comte de Sparre, produce classic Moulin-à-Vent: rich, robust and structured, and well worth seeking out.

Good Moulin-à-Vent producers

Jean Pierre Bloud (Chateau du Moulin-à-Vent)
Chauvet Frères
Domaine Jacky Janodet
Domaine Lemonon (Loron & Fils)
Raymond Siffert (Domaine de la Bruyère)
Domaine de la Tour du Bief (Comte de Sparre)

FLEURIE

This is the favourite wine of the Beaujolais at present, to such an extent that its price has now overtaken that of Moulin-à-Vent – more a reflection of the pretty name, one feels, than the innate superiority of the product. Like Chablis, it is easy to pronounce, and

The top Beaujolais cru *of Moulin-à-Vent takes its name not from a village but from this now sail-less windmill on the outskirts of Romanèche-Thorins.*

this helps transatlantic sales enormously. It can also boast a commendable degree of consistency in its style, with obvious fruit and the aromatic charm its name suggests. The wines are rarely given the chance to show what they can achieve with bottle age.

With 780 hectares producing about 465,000 cases per annum one might think that supplies are good, but to judge by the rising prices, it looks as if demand is greater. If any *cru* can be singled out as epitomizing Beaujolais, then Fleurie is the one – but it may not necessarily offer the best value for money. The Cave Coopérative is of particular significance here in that it is responsible for the vinification of around 30 per cent of the entire production of this, the third largest of the individual *crus* of Beaujolais.

Good Fleurie producers
Maurice Bruone, Montgénas (Eventail)
Cave Coopérative
Michel Chignard
Dr Darroze, Domaine des Quatre Vents (Duboeuf)
Château de Grand Pré (Ferraud)
Domaine de la Presle (André Barraud)

CHIROUBLES

The 350 hectares of Chiroubles vineyards, situated at around the 400 metre mark, are the highest in altitude of all the *crus*, a factor which contributes to its lightness of style. The wines of this commune lie at the opposite end of the vinous spectrum from those of nearby Moulin-à-Vent, and are the first of all the *crus* to achieve maturity, usually being ready for bottling and consumption by the February or March following the vintage. Some 195,000 cases are produced annually of this light-hearted, unserious wine: the most pretty and precocious of all the ten Beaujolais *crus*.

On my first ever visit to Chiroubles, in the days when a full stomach was more important than a comfortable bed, I spent the night in my car on a remote lane above the village, only to be woken from a light sleep at about four-thirty a.m. by an energetic *vigneron* going off on his tractor to spray his vines before the heat of the sun made the work harder. I hope, and suspect, that the same *vigneron* took his reward at midday with a generous *pichet* of young Chiroubles followed by a siesta! The Beaujolais hills become distinctly sleepy by mid-afternoon. Not for nothing

This bleak view of Fleurie shows the gobelet-*trained Gamay vines starkly visible in the foreground. The bare winter landscape contrasts strongly with the rich foliage of summer.*

does one estate here sell some of its wine under the name of 'Grille-Midi'.

The land up here is steeper and harder to work than anywhere else in Beaujolais, and life has not always been as easy and profitable as it seems to be now for the growers of Chiroubles. They are riding the crest of a wave at present, with their wines selling in Paris at prices almost as high as those asked for Fleurie. By June the best cellars here are empty.

Good Chiroubles producers

Domaine Bouillard
Domaine Cheysson-les-Farges
Maison des Vignerons (Cave Coopérative)
Bernard Méziat
Domaine du Moulin (André Depré)
Georges Passot (Domaine de la Grosse Pierre)
Château de Raousset (Duboeuf)

MORGON

With 1,030 hectares stretching between Fleurie and
Brouilly, Morgon produces on average some
610,000 cases annually, making it the second largest
of all the *crus*. The full name of the commune is in
fact Villié-Morgon, after its largest village.

It is not easy to generalize about the character of
Morgon wines since there is considerable soil variation within the appellation. The best soils lie on the
Côte de Py, a ridge lying between the two villages of
Morgon and Villié-Morgon, and it is from here that
the best wines come. Much of Villié-Morgon,
though, produces lighter wine and indeed some is
only entitled to the Beaujolais-Villages appellation.

The best soils are distinguished by decomposing
schist known as *roche-pourrie* (rotten rock) and it is
this, together with certain minerals, which gives
some Morgon wines their ability to develop a particular style with age. This peculiarity has even led to
the coining of the verb *morgonner* to describe the
acquisition of the flavour. When young, Morgon is
more charming than Moulin-à-Vent, yet it seems to
age just as well, often better. The 1985 Morgon in
my cellar at present has the distinctive aroma of
griotte cherries often found in the wines of this *cru*.
But it is true to say that there are two styles of Morgon now: some are truly individual and characteristic
of Morgon itself, while others are indistinguishable
from the anodyne monostyle that is common in many
lesser wines from the Beaujolais *crus*.

Good Morgon producers

Jean Descombes
Louis Desvignes
Sylvain Fessy (Cuvée André Gauthier)
Louis Genillon (Eventail)
Domaine des Pillets (Gérard Brisson)
Domaine de Ruyère (Paul Collonge)
Domaine Savoye

RÉGNIÉ

Régnié, bracketed with its neighbour Durette, is due
to make the transition to *cru* status, its wines having
for some time earned a slightly higher price than the
average for Beaujolais-Villages. Such an elevation
seems deserved, since the wines here are often similar
in style and quality to those of the adjacent Brouilly,
but I have yet to taste Régnié wines that can compete
with the very best in Beaujolais. From 560 hectares
of vineyards, it produces around 30,000 hectolitres
annually.

Good Régnié producers

Desplace Frères
Jean & Yves Durand
Roland Magrin (Domaine de la Gerarde)
Joël Rochette
Château de la Tour Bourdon

BROUILLY

The appellation of Brouilly covers 12,000 hectares
and produces around 750,000 cases per annum,
making it the largest of all the *crus*. As such its wines
should not prove hard to find. The vineyards are
dominated by an extinct volcano, Mont Brouilly,
which stands in their midst, 484 metres high, in iso-
lation from the main *massif* of the Beaujolais hills.
There is no actual village of Brouilly as such, and six
different communes are permitted to use the appellation: Odenas, Cercié and St Lager, and parts of
Quincié, Charentay and St Etienne-la-Varenne. At
their basic level of quality, the wines are scarcely
worth more than the excellent Beaujolais-Villages
produced in, for example, the other parts of Quincié
or St Etienne-des-Ouillières. But the best wines,
from producers such as those listed below, do have
authority and merit their *cru* status.

There are a number of unusually large properties
within the appellation, with grand châteaux that
remind one of Bordeaux rather than Burgundy. But
with the system of *métayage* prevalent in Beaujolais
(see page 69), the perplexing situation arises whereby many growers make wine from the same property
and produce different wines under the same name.
This means that there is less consistency here than in
some of the other *crus*. Nevertheless, the general
standard is good and Brouilly wines are worthy
ambassadors for the satisfying and uncomplicated
style of Beaujolais. They do not usually benefit from
ageing for more than two or three years.

Good Brouilly producers

Château du Bluizard (Duboeuf)
Château de la Chaize
Domaine de Combillaty (Duboeuf)
Robert Condemine
Georges Dutraive
Robert Farjat
Claudius Geoffray
Château de Pierreux
André Ronzière (Eventail)
Jean-Paul Ruet

The rolling hills of the Bas-Beaujolais stretch away to the south of the Côte de Brouilly.

CÔTE DE BROUILLY

The vineyards here lie entirely on the slopes of the more-or-less circular Mont Brouilly and thus enjoy the spectrum of exposure from north to south to east to west. If Brouilly was a single appellation, then Côte de Brouilly would rank as a Premier Cru, for its wines generally possess more strength and concentration. In fact its minimum permitted natural alcohol level of ten-and-a-half degrees is half-a-degree higher than that of the other *crus*. It was the growers here with vines on the slopes of this extinct volcano who campaigned successfully for a special appellation to distinguish their wines from those of the surrounding countryside at the foot of Mont Brouilly.

Côte de Brouilly produces around 170,000 cases from its 300 hectares, but as the vineyards have such a variety of exposure, the wines are likely to be less consistent in style than those from an appellation with a more homogeneous aspect. Thus in certain years, some slopes will perform better than others. In hot summers, those on the steep, well-drained, south face may experience excessive heat and drought, while those high up the hill and facing north will retain better natural acidity and consequently more intense fruit and a finer structure. At times, a Côte de Brouilly from these slopes even seems to have something in common with white wines such as Sancerre. "Of course," a good grower said to me one day when I remarked on this. "It's the only Gamay wine with the flavour of Sauvignon Blanc." This could be explained by a combination of high altitude and northern exposure. Wines coming from the southern slopes are likely to be more robust.

Another idiosyncrasy here is in the soil. The pink granite which is the hallmark of the other *crus* gives way in places to the *pierre bleue*, a blue granite of comparatively recent volcanic origins, which adds a touch of complexity and finesse to the normally straightforward wines of the appellation.

Good Côte de Brouilly producers
Domaine de Chavannes (Claudius Geoffray)
André Large (Eventail)
Château Thivin
Lucien & Robert Verger (Vignoble de L'Ecluse)

BEAUJOLAIS-VILLAGES

These are the best buy of all in Beaujolais at the moment. The wines come from the Haut-Beaujolais and can on occasion rival those of the *crus*, especially from low-yielding old vines on a good steep south-facing slope. As for the cost, it is usually not a great deal more than for basic Beaujolais, and it is significantly less than for the more famous of the *crus*, whose prices seem nowadays to follow in the slipstream of Côte d'Or burgundies.

Styles can vary considerably according to the

Good Beaujolais and Beaujolais-Villages producers
There are eighteen cooperatives in the entire region, and all produce very acceptable and honest wines. In addition, you will be in good hands with any of the Beaujolais *négociants-éleveurs* listed opposite. The Eventail de Vignerons Producteurs is an association of high-quality growers who collaborate to bottle and market their individual wines, and this, too, is a name well-worth looking out for.
If you want individual growers' wines that have been estate bottled, then the best place to start is by looking in the better villages. The following should not disappoint.
Charles Brechard, Le Bois d'Oingt
Jean-Marc Charmet, Le Breuil
Domaine de Chêne (André Jaffre), Charentay
Paul Gauthier, Blacé
Edmond Giloux, Leynes
Pierre Jomard, Fleurieux-sur-l'Arbresle
Claude & Michelle Joubert, Lantignié
Château de Lacarelle, St Etienne-des-Oullières
Bernard Mera, Marchampt
René Miolane, Salles-en-Beaujolais
Maurice Perroud, Lantignié
Domaine de La Sorbière (Jean-Charles Pivot), Quincié
Jean Verger, Blacé

nature of the soil in the vineyard. In some places there is a good deal of sand, making for relatively light and forward wines with elegance but not a lot of stuffing. In others, where there is more granite, you can find considerable depth and power in the wines, even sometimes an uncanny hint of Pinot Noir, and this characteristic becomes more developed in the wines as they acquire age.

Up to four million cases are produced annually from around 6,000 hectares (14,500 acres) with a maximum permitted yield of fifty hectolitres per hectare. Good villages include Régnié (due to be elevated to *cru* status as from 1988), Lantignié, Quincié, Marchampt, St Etienne-des-Oullières, Le Perréon, Blacé.

BEAUJOLAIS

Simple Beaujolais is best drunk within France itself, and best of all in Beaujolais, before it has been subjected to the shock of a bottling line. Most light red wines lose much of their charm when stabilized for the shelves of supermarkets all over the world, and Beaujolais is no exception. Customers abroad would do well to forget simple Beaujolais, apart from the better Nouveau wines. They are less attractive and offer less good value for money than Beaujolais-Villages. Between five and six million cases are produced annually from around 9,000 hectares (22,000 acres), and the maximum permitted yield is fifty-five hectolitres per hectare, though as always this may be raised by the INAO if the vintage warrants. Le Bois d'Oingt is a particularly good area, but this district is more strongly influenced by the presence of co-operatives and *negoçiants* than by considerations of *terroir*. Mostly lying to the south of Villefranche, the district accounts for up to half the total production of the whole Beaujolais region, and probably for over three-quarters of all Nouveau.

Recommended Beaujolais Négociants-Eleveurs
Jacques Dépagneux, Villefranche-sur-Saône
Georges Duboeuf, Romanèche-Thorins
Pierre Ferraud, Belleville
Sylvain Fessy (Vins Dessalle), Belleville
Trénel Fils, Charnay-lès-Mâcon
Other reliable names include the following:
Chauvet Frères, La Chapelle-de-Guinchay
Chanut Frères, Romanèche-Thorins
Loron & Fils, Pontanevaux
Louis Tête, St Didier-sur-Beaujeu

INDEX

ACKNOWLEDGEMENTS

The Publishers thank the following for providing the photographs in
this book:

Antony Blake Photo Library 64; Michael Busselle 76; Hubrecht Duijker 1,
2/3, 24, 52, 73, 74; Patrick Eager 33, 66; Explorer (F. Jalain) 8/9; French
Picture Library (Barrie Smith) 14; Robert Harding Picture Library 16;
Maison Marie Claire (Planchard) 38; Photographer's Library (Michael
Busselle) 45; Picturepoint 39, 58; Tony Stone Associates (Thierry
Cazabon) 46/7, 56, 60, (John Wyand) 18; Top Agence (Pascal Hinous) 48,
54, (Pierre Putelat) 42, (J-N Reichel) 21; Topham Picture Library 23; Zefa
Picture Library (R. Bond) 36/7, (Colin Maher) 71.

Editor: Andrew Jefford
Art Editor: Bob Gordon
Designer: Ted Kinsey
Picture Research: Angela Grant

Maps: Russell Barnett
Grape illustrations: Nicki Kemball
represented by John Hodgson